COUNTRY JOURNAL
&
OLD MAN'S MUSINGS

Ken M. Blomberg

Ten|16
PRESS

www.ten16press.com - Waukesha, WI

For information, please contact:

www.ten16press.com
Waukesha, WI

Cover Drawing - "Buster" by artist Bob Bertram (2022)
Sketches throughout - by the author

Back Page - Photo of the Author - by Dave Engel

This book is dedicated to the memory of "Buster," my beloved gun dog and sidekick for twelve and a half years, who passed while writing this book.

FOREWORD

"On the way to the marshes this evening I paused to sit for a while with old Matt Mettel on his car seat south of his house along the river. He pointed to the blossoming locusts and said 'When the locusts bloom, then it is time to plant the corn. Then it's warm enough.' He went on to speak of locust wood. 'Ain't nothing better next to cedar than locust. You bet! Beats oak any time. I'd just as soon have locust as oak-even as cedar." *He continued in this vein for half an hour, as mellow as the evening air."*

August Derleth - Countryman's Journal - June 1st entry

Derleth's words in his 1963 book were my inspiration to keep a journal throughout the year, so beginning in June of 2022 I began assembling my thoughts and inspirations. This is my journey around the sun as a seasoned outdoor writer. Daily entries, month to month, season to season, interspersed with periodic musings and notable quotes. A year's worth of observations. A diary, so to speak. A grandfather's look at grown children, grandchildren, mothers, fathers, neighbors, friends and strangers. And dogs. A kennel full of dogs. A reflection on a lifetime of owning and loving gun dogs.

And nature's notes. From my perch on 45 acres in central

Wisconsin, I bring to you the end result of fifty years of observations. Still learning. Oh, there's so much to learn. It was Einstein who said, "We still do not know one thousandth of one percent of what nature has revealed to us." And a day does not go by that I don't learn something out my back door on the land our family has owned for more than four decades.

My writing career can be traced back to Greendale High school's newspaper. English teacher Mrs. Nehring assigned me to sports reporting. Football, basketball and baseball games were my beat. Keeping score and describing game highlights was my assignment. I earned, but have since lost a lapel pin badge of honor.

In an English class in the mid-70s at state college in central Wisconsin, Professor Shumway gave me an A for an essay I wrote on deer hunting. One of very few As earned in four years of higher education. I was hooked on writing from that day forward. Success in English courses prompted me to try my hand at freelance writing. After graduating with a B.S. degree in Resource Management and finding employment in my field I continued to write on the side. My first published article in a regional weekly outdoor newspaper landed me $4.80 back in 1979. Subsequently, I discovered I had a talent for putting words on paper and that fact was acknowledged when my articles were accepted by the likes of national magazines Field & Stream, Fur, Fish & Game, Wing & Shot and RGS Drummer - as well as state publications like Wisconsin Sportsman, Badger Sportsman, and Woods and Waters.

Writing was and still is my passion and a day does not go by without it being on my agenda. In the 80s I began writing a monthly magazine gun dog column, "Kennel Talk", which I continued to write for more than twenty years until recently, when the same magazine, Badger Sportsman fell on hard times.

In the 90s I created a weekly newspaper outdoor column, "Up the Creek", which ran for years in several central Wisconsin weekly newspapers - the Plover Profile, Manawa Advocate and the Tomorrow River Times. In 2006, the column was picked up by Gannett Wisconsin Newspapers in the Wausau, Stevens Point, Marshfield and Wisconsin Rapids markets. After Gannett restructured their community newspapers, I was asked by the editor of the local Portage County Gazette to write my outdoor column for their weekly newspaper.

Besides weekly newspaper columns, I continued to write freelance outdoor pieces for state and national magazines. I published the first of three books - Up the Creek, Ten16 Press (2017), Wisconsin Bird Hunting Tales, The History Press (2018) and Letters from Art, Ten16 Press (2019). This book, *Country Journal and Old Man Musings*, Ten16 press (2024) was completed while I continued to work on my first novel, Chequamegon! Moon River.

And I'd be remiss to not mention that for the past decade or so, I've been a member of the Mid-State Towers, a small monthly gathering of poets, writers and musicians. Participating in this long-standing, unsung group of great literary minds has been a wonderful inspiration in this old man's writing, musings and yes, poetry.

My wife, the "boss", two grown sons, two wonderful daughter-in-laws and four precious grandchildren make up my immediate family and daily inspirations. Extended relatives, close friends and neighbors also comprise an expanded circle of individuals that have shaped my life.

This book is for my present family, and other family members in the future who I may never meet or know. Perhaps, some day they too, may understand my obsession with the land we share with the creatures inhabiting the surrounding woods, fields and waters. It's a companion to my first book, *Up the Creek*, and God willing, the first of several future *Country Journals and Old Man Musings.*

I have a lot more to say and learn.

Ken M. Blomberg
Town of Eau Pleine 2024

THE WINDOW TO MY WORLD

*It measures approximately 6 feet
wide by 4 feet high. It's the window to my daily
world. Facing to the east, it welcomes the sun in the morning,
oversees daytime activities in the prairie grass field and pond, and
watches over elongated, late afternoon shadows, engulfed by the woods.*

*I gaze over my keyboard screen and look skyward, often spotting soaring eagles,
vultures, hawks and occasional flocks of geese and ducks. Movement in the
tall prairie grass might reveal deer browsing or passing to the neighbor's
corn and soybean fields to the north. Songbirds of many stripes visit
the feeders and birdhouses mounted on the deck handrails.*

*It's my window to daily weather reports. Clouds carrying
rain, snow, thunder and lightning pass by, and only
stop long enough to allow clear, blue skies to
prevail. And when I crank open two side
windows, fresh air surrounds me
and clears my senses.*

Woke up on the recliner in the house this morning. A nasty head cold was still present. I haven't had a good night's sleep for a week. The boss suspects I've acquired allergies to pollen in my old age. She's probably right. A lifetime of allergies has made her an expert in pollen counts, remedies and suffering. So nasal sprays, a pill for allergy relief and a couple of doses of inhaler and I'm good to go. I guess.

A dog is scheduled to check in this morning at 8 am, so out to the kennel I go at 7:30. The indoor cockers followed me around the prairie field for their morning constitutional. The local flock of Canada geese numbered 18 this morning as they flew over the house. Yesterday, the flock numbered just shy of one hundred! This time of the year large gatherings represent juvenile birds. Adults are waterbound now, tending to this year's crop of goslings.

Number 2 son is working this morning and on Saturday in Wausau, but plans on staying here for the night. Said he'll help bury a drain pipe from the kennel to the pond this afternoon. I've prepared the trench already with the tractor and plow, so laying and burying the pipe should be easy enough. After morning kennel chores, I plan on cutting grass with the garden tractor - a couple hour task.

It's 8:30 and no sign of my 8 am boarder, so here I sit at my office desk making an entry in the JOURNAL and writing an OLD MAN MUSING. The drugs seem to have kicked in.

IF I WERE A RIVER

If I were a river,
I'd flow on forever.
Never look back,
Always face forward.
Seldom pause to reflect,
Never worry about dying.

If I were a cloud,
I'd fancy myself a cumulus.
Not a fat, rotund one.
Rather a lean, mean
preceding a storm type.
Floating by at 1,000 feet,
throwing shadows on fields below.
Powder white in the middle,
gray around the edges.
Ready to pour forth when met
with backward flowing low fronts,
Recharging rivers below.

If I were a river,
I'd watch the skies
above for clouds.
For clouds are my
lifeblood. Without which,
I'd cease to flow and die.

Granddaughter Number 1 broke her arm yesterday. In reality it was her elbow that shattered from a fall from the monkey bars at her school's playground. School's out, but she and her brothers were killing time while their mother, an elementary teacher at their school, worked after hours. At urgent care, the technicians examining the x-rays gasped out loud. "We knew it was bad," her mother later exclaimed. The eight foot fall did the job and finding a surgeon skilled enough to repair the damage proved difficult. But one was found in Marshfield and surgery was scheduled for next week. A temporary sling and immobilizing wrap would have to suffice until then.

This was her second arm break. The first, two years past, involved a climb in a tree and fall onto exposed roots. Peyton is a climber. Trees in our woods are a challenge she takes on whenever time allows. The woodpile out back is a favorite mountain to climb. Logs up to ten feet long, haphazardly piled in a forgotten garden beckon her and her brothers every time they visit.

It's a wonder she hasn't broken something there, or in our woods over the years. Better though, while under supervision of her parents rather than her grandparents!

MOMENTS IN TIME

As simple as a babbling creek,
As mundane as a bee gathering sweet nectar,
As lonesome as a distant barking dog at night,
As satisfying as the last cup of morning coffee on the deck,
Or the view you've gazed over the prairie field for the thousandth time.
As beautiful as a dew drenched spider web reflected in morning sun,
Sparkling ripples in the creek,
Whispering music from pine needles in the wind,
And the look from my bird dog as he stares into my eyes.

Where does it come from?
Where does it go?
Beyond my comprehension.
Past memories from years gone by.
Today's reflections.
Moments in time that fill our lives.
Yesterday. Today. Tomorrow.
Embrace and cherish them.
Before they pass you by.

June 12

Hope the statutes of limitations include the plucking of lilac suckers. That's just what I did maybe 15 years ago at a nearby wildlife area and on the roadside by John Muir's family homestead near Montello. Well, the fruits of those tiny roots finally bore forth this year when the fragrant flowers blossomed and graced our front yard and airspace.

June 13

Mowing trails through the woods and around the pond and prairie field today. It's a monthly chore - more often, sometimes weekly, if rain falls on a more regular basis. That is the case this year. While mowing lately, I noticed our wild flowers are blooming like crazy. Do they bloom in color coordination? Why does it seem white flowers precede yellow and purple? Or is it just me?

Insects - bees, butterflies, dragonflies and a multitude of others - are working the field like an army bent on victory. Working against time, they flit from flower to flower, leaf to leaf, plant to plant, all day long. Rain slows them down, but only a downpour stops production. Before the last drop of rain hits the ground, they're at it again.

Busy as bees. So the saying goes.

June 14

Lone doe deer have been dropping this year's fawns. When disturbed, or feeding in nearby fields, they run off, leaving their fawn curled up in grass or forest litter with instructions to stay put. "Don't move a muscle. Don't blink an eye or twitch an ear," mother warns. "Rest assured, I'll be back for you." We humans must heed mother doe. Do not disturb the fawn. It has not been abandoned.

June 15

I'm no scrooge, but I now know an Ebenezer. And a Stuttgarter. The former is white, the latter yellow. Both are onions. I planted these two varieties in one of our raised bed garden boxes this year. "Thin out the radishes," warned the boss. Alongside tomato, pepper, and cucumber plants occupying other backyard boxes, our modest garden this year should bear vegetables in the weeks and months ahead.

The cockers encountered a family of turkeys in our two-acre food plot at the end of our ten-acre prairie grass field last evening. On their evening "poop run", Mitzi flushed the hen and a pair of quail-sized chicks, who all took flight towards the woods along the creek. Subsequently, eight more chicks flew and scattered in all directions. Buster saw the action transpire from the confines of the hedgerow on the north side of the food plot. There, he was finishing his evening constitutional, but launched into the fray of turkey mayhem.

From my perch in the UTV Ranger, I hollered the come command. Buster obliged first and loaded into the rear dog crate. Mitzi however, took more time to unwind the temptation to chase, but eventually joined her father in the kennel box. I'm happy to report, nor harm came to the chicks and hen.

SIT A SPELL

I will sit a spell by the river edge,
And gaze upon its sparkling reflection.
Hear cascading water falling over a ledge,
And listen as waves lap upon shoreline deflection.

From my home porch I will listen to birdsong,
Hear a dove's mournful cooing greet the sun,
and blackbirds angrily protecting cattail nests at dawn,
While cranes trumpet across the gravel road to everyone.

Orioles and cardinals flash brilliant colors,
Against the drab brown berry choked hedgerow.
And a woodcock still dances on his evening singing cover.
Nature's sights and melodies are soothing for the soul you know.

Day two of a nasty heat wave. Heat advisory issued for the second day in a row. 90-something with 70-something humidity. Too hot to run the dogs farther than the pond and back to the kennel. But Josh called yesterday and wanted to come down to work for a while today. "Sure," I replied. "Come here and we'll bury a drain pipe from the kennel to the pond. Come early before it gets too hot to work."

So we laid 300 feet of 3-inch pipe, connected it to the rain barrels that catch water off the roof. Tested it with a garden hose and by golly, it worked. Now, I'm hoping for rain.

June 25

The boss's bird feeders were destroyed for a second time this summer. Suspected culprit was a bear. That was verified, as a sow bear and her two cubs tripped one of our trail cameras after 9 pm last night. Proof by pictures from the one set up near Golden Pond. And speaking of pictures, the first trail photos of bucks sprouting velvet antlers have appeared.

A neighbor's young daughter Zelda, started working at the boarding kennel today. She replaces the Pumper boys, who "retired" last year after six years of dedicated service. Cleaning kennels and tending dogs is a never ending process, and this old man certainly appreciates the help.

"He is richest who is content with the least,
for content is the wealth of nature."
~Socrates

June 27

Mowing trails around the 10-acre prairie field always yields a story or two. Today's surprise was mama hen turkey and her 10 chicks, once again near the food plot. Upon further inspection of the grassland floor found an abundant crop of ground insects - a great source of high protein to jump start these young gallinaceous birds. By September, these youngsters will weigh 10 - 15 pounds. That's a lot of grasshoppers, slugs and caterpillars!

July 2

Neighbors Paul and Steve paraded a large, black Amish draft horse past our house and down the road this morning. After talking to Steve later on the phone, we learned that the beast of a horse was on the loose and had headed into the swampy woods northeast of our place. Granddaughter Peyton and I joined the rodeo on our Ranger UTV and traveled around the nine square mile block of woods down River and Dam Roads. To no avail, but we stopped and visited with three neighbors and caught up on local gossip.

Learned later that the horse was finally caught 3 miles north along Dam Road.

July 3

A day on the lake. Number 2 son and family brought the family pontoon today for a cruise on nearby Lake Dubay. Holiday weekends bring out the crowds, but we launched early and after a 6-hour trip across the 6,600 acre flowage we departed after many had left. My dad loved Dubay, and after he and mom retired in Wausau, his boat was moored there for many years until his death. "I like the fact that despite the large crowds attracted there on weekends, they spread out quite comfortably. Nothing like southern Wisconsin lakes on weekends!" he reflected.

Anyway, on this day, our family found quiet spots to swim, fish and enjoy dinner on the boat from a local tavern on the lake, Dock of Dubay. The weather was perfect, the grandchildren behaved, but unfortunately, the fish weren't biting. Another day in paradise.

July 5

One and a half inches of rain yesterday. Last month's work on the rainwater pipeline paid off, as nearly 2,232 gallons ran off the kennel's metal roof, through the gutters, into rain barrels and by garden hose into the 3 inch pipe we buried 300 feet east to Vera's Pond. I wonder if the roof runoff will make a difference. It certainly can't hurt.

THE WIND

Sitting on the back porch with the boss yesterday I gazed skyward and watched small, scattered stratus clouds racing to the southeast. Following another wave of severe thunderstorms the night before, our rain gauge told the story. We had been spared more rain, wind damage and power outages that occurred north and south of our place along the creek.

The speeding clouds brought a song to mind. It was Bob Dylan's 1962 classic, Blowin' in the Wind. "How many times must a man look up before he can see the sky? The answer, my friend, is blowin' in the wind."

I dare you to look at the lyrics of this 60 year old song.

Then reach with me for answers about freedom and death.

In his book, A Sand County Almanac, the great conservationist and hunter

Aldo Leopold listened to geese and wind "blowing taps for summer".
He watched geese disappear on southerly
winds and dreamed he could too, "If I were the wind".
Do yourself a favor and read, or re-read his Almanac.
His land ethic includes words of wisdom on human ethics -
both in short supply these days.
Henry David Thoreau speculated that when things were at loose ends,
"Who knows which way the wind will blow tomorrow?"
John Muir once said, "The winds will blow their own freshness into you,
and the storms their energy, while cares will drop away from you
like the leaves of Autumn."
Thoreau, reminded us, "The morning wind forever blows,
the poem of creation is uninterrupted;
but few have the ears to hear it."
So, during these troubled times I urge you to stop what you're doing
and from time to time turn your face into the wind, close your eyes
and listen. Your answers my friends, might just be blowin' in the wind.

July 9

River Road, a mile east of our home, was the original wagon track of the pioneers - a trail for Native Americans, settlers, fur traders, lumbermen and travelers to the wilderness of Wisconsin's northwoods. Look hard enough and you can still see the remnants of a footpath right along the river's bank. Three miles north, both tracts encountered John Dubay's trading post and ferry on the east side of the river and a short cut to another road heading north. Today, River Road stands testament to the area's history. When travel and life was slower and more deliberate. So much has changed, yet the whiskey colored river still flows by - steady as she goes.

FAVORITE PASTIMES

Two of my favorite pastimes
are watching clouds float by
while sitting the kennel deck
and water flow past my perch
on the nearby river bank.

Both represent segments of
Nature's water cycle. One as
vaporized crystals, lighter than
air, the other, excess droplets
combined to run off the
landscape downstream to
thirsty oceans.

Whatever their motive, they both
never cease to entertain this seeker
of tranquility and peace.
Job well done!

July 12

The kids took a walk on the dike that holds back Wisconsin River water at Dubay last night. They stopped and swam at "Erik's Beach", a sandy shoreline at the base of rocky granite fill that prevents erosion from waves off the 6,600 acre flowage. On a clear day one can spot Rib Mountain, twenty-some miles to the north. On a calm day, this beach provides ample entertainment for youngsters and adults alike. Our kids range in age from 2 to 39 years. That makes Nina and Papa old-timers - now that we're pushing 70! We've lived 44 years below the dike.

July 15

Sold the outdoor wood burning boiler today. It served us well for 10 years. Sat silent last winter, as we replaced it with a LP boiler serving the kennel's in-floor heating system. The wood-burning Lopi stove in the house's living room kept us warm enough, with a basement forced air furnace as backup on real cold snaps. Selling the outdoor boiler was bittersweet. But this old man met its match. Burned 15 full cords the last season of its use. Loading that beast several times a day got the better of me. Especially when it was late on a snowy evening in windy, below zero weather.

Our Lopi is now on the market, as in a couple of weeks a brand new pellet stove is scheduled for installation in our living room. Last time I checked, a pellet weighs less than a log.

July 18

The Lopi left our home and went to Tomahawk today. 81 year-old Loyd and his wife Josie picked up the 400 pound wood-stove, with the help of a hand cart, ratchet straps and No. 2 son Karl and the family's John Deere tractor forklift. A new pellet stove is due to arrive by the end of the month.

July 20

Welcome relief in the weather this morning. A cold front from the northwest blew away high humidity and heavy dew points. We gathered on the front porch and enjoyed the heavenly breeze and 70 degree temperatures. A far cry from recent 90s. As the rest of the world bakes and burns, we rejoice in Wisconsin's climate. Knock on wood. September can't arrive any time soon.

WIND SONGS

Does the sound come from pine
needles or the wind?
In a gentle breeze it's but a whisper.
Stronger winds spawn a song.

Gales of November
make them roar.
Without the wind they
remain quiet.

Without needles they
stand silent.
But together, their songs
touch our souls.

Nature' s wind songs tell
stories to those listening
At times, above human
comprehension.
So stop, listen, and read
between the lines.

July 23

Eagle River. Spent the last two days in this northern Wisconsin community. There, the Trees For Tomorrow environmental education camp hosted the Wisconsin Outdoor Communicators Association (WOCA) annual conference. A cookout, sessions on wolf and bear management, wilderness dog sledding trips, women in the outdoors, political interference in the outdoors, outdoor writer comradery and lamenting on our profession - a dying breed.

Wildflowers, butterflies and bluestem grasses. Ever present and engulfing the back 40 prairie field. Reports of a drop in monarch butterflies has me looking closely at local numbers. Last week, the International Union for the Conservation of Nature reported "migrating monarch butterflies have moved closer to extinction in the past decade - prompting scientists to officially designate them as 'endangered'". Plenty of milkweed plants growing throughout the field, but no caterpillars? Butterflies? Yes, several species, but by no means abundant. Stay tuned, maybe August will tell another story.

WHERE DID THEY GO?

"Where are the pollinators?", I asked myself.
Across our homestead's prairie grasslands
the flowers bloomed, the grasses ripened,
and the dragonflies and swallows fed.
But where were the bugs?
Daily trips along the trails bordering the
field and along the planted hedgerow
revealed a gloomy picture of pollinator numbers.

But wait. Today I paused at several locations
on the ten-acre field, in full prairie flower bloom -
Coneflowers, Aster, and ox eyed daisies. Stop
and look closer. Dozens of smaller, less
prominent species of wildflowers were present,
laying low and less conspicuous. Milkweed

and Mullins poked their flowering heads above
the denser bluestem and goldenrod.

And lo and behold, stop, look and concentrate.
I began seeing a host of small butterflies,
bees and other low flying nectar gathering bugs.

Even with an abundance of milkweed plants
distributed across the field, I saw very few
monarch butterflies.
Maybe they're late this year and August will
bring them forth. Just wait.

August 5

"If the first week in August is unusually warm, the winter will be white and long." Richard Inwards - Weather Lore.

If that's the case this year, batten down the hatches. Above normal temperatures this July have bled into the first week of this month. So, according to lore, we may be in store for lots of snow and winter hanging on longer than normal. Time will tell.

August 6

National weather forecasts are calling for continued heat advisories across ⅔ of the country and our heat index today is pushing 97 degrees. Thank goodness for air conditioning. The small portable one in my kennel office barely keeps up, but allows me to work in the morning at my desk writing. I'm afraid I'll have to go to the house where the central air conditioning maintains a comfort level we enjoy. The dogs remain in their indoor kennel space, which is well ventilated with fans. The good news is a cold front is forecast to arrive tonight from the north. However, relief comes with thunderstorms and much needed rain.

Well, the past two night's cold fronts brought mild storms and rain. 2 ¼ inches total. Potentially, five thousand gallons off the kennel roof and down the drain pipe to the pond. Upon inspection, the pond's water level was up a bit. But still way below high levels.

"If a robin sings on a high branch of a tree, it is a sign of fine weather; but if one sings near the ground, the weather will be wet."
~Oswestry

Perhaps that's why our backyard robins have been ground bound the past few days and haven't flown beyond the lowest tree branches of late.

POND LIFE

*Life on the pond
is easy going.
Tadpoles mind their
own business
until they meet the
likes of herons,
mink, or grandchildren.
Blackbirds build nests
in the cattails,
where they raise young
and ward off
hawks and crows.*

*Dragonflies and
swallows feast on
flying insects hatching*

by the hours. But
for decoys like geese
and ducks it's a
matter of random drift.
A life of Riley.
Not a care in the world.

When the wind
comes from the
north, they hang out
along the south
shore. An easterly
blow sends them
west. And from the
west they go east.

When the wind
comes from the south,
they hang out along
the north shore.

Such is the leisure of
untethered decoys.

August 12

The kennel is full of boarders and personal dogs. Boarding are a beagle, a lab mix and two Lagotto Romagnolos. What in the world are Lagotto Romagnolos? Italian water dogs, according to the experts, "Italy's adorable 'truffle dog' sports a curly coat and lavish facial furnishings. Despite their plush-toy looks, Lagotti are durable workers of excellent noses who root out truffles, a dainty and pricey delicacy."

Three days and counting! That's the countdown to the arrival of our offspring from Maine. No. 1 son, his wife and our No. 2 grandson. The phone rang yesterday afternoon and it was none other than Carson, our blond haired 5-year old grandson who we only see in person about once a year. "The three things I can't wait to do are play with my cousins, swim and see Nina. Oh, and Papa too."

This year's visit coincides with a family gathering on a Waushara County lake called Iragomi. The kids will swim, boat and fish until they drop. The adults will posture on the dock and deck while talk will skirt family matters and politics - then I'll have to excuse myself to matters back at the kennel. "Gotta go!" I'll fib.

THE OLDER I GET

The older I get the more I sit.
I sit to fish, on shore and in my boat.
My duck blind bench supports my bottom,
and a folding camo chair accompanies me,
pothole to pothole.
In the uplands, while following my dogs down
trails, I look for stumps, fallen logs and boulders.
Resting along the way adds time to the hunt
and rests my weary legs.

By the river without gun or rod, I like to perch my
backside on her banks.
I watch the water pass by, a few days
out of Mosinee, Tomahawk, or
Rhinelander.

Three Ravens flew over my duck blind the other day. They growled as they passed, and triggered a crow to join the raspy music. Ten minutes later they returned for a second verse.

I smiled when I realized why I noticed. The older I get, the more I sit.

Another countdown. In seventeen days, the 2022 hunting season begins in Wisconsin. Those of us afflicted with the urge to hunt, fish and spend time out of doors react to dates on the calendar that mark the beginning of our seasons. September is the first month of autumn. Migration of birds is well underway for many songbirds. Bird feeder activity is the first to show telltale signs. Game birds like blue and green wing teal, morning doves and Canada geese flock up and begin their process of heading south. Hunters take to their blinds and revel in the changing seasons.

GRAY HAIR

I looked in the mirror and there I was.
I stared as an old man looked back.

Gray hair replaced brown on top, wrinkles etched
once smoother skin. Bags under eyes, folds
between brows and lashes.
Whiskers growing long below my cheeks.

Eyes of blue, bloodshot and searching.
Looking back at a lifetime of wonder.
Looking ahead at things to come.

Life is like that.
Looking back and forth
at the same time.

I looked in the mirror and
the man I once knew was gone.

Family gatherings. In the midst of the second one this summer. No. 1 son and family flew into Wisconsin this week from Maine where he and his wife Sabrina and son Carson live and work at the state university. No. 2 son and family from nearby Coloma are here. Here, in the family Eau Pleine homestead - now housing all ten of us. Thank goodness we built on twenty years ago with a second story complete with 4 rooms and two bathrooms upstairs and a master bedroom and two bathrooms downstairs. Even with that, grandmother and two grandchildren slept in the overflow travel trailer parked and hooked up in the backyard. Day 3 of a week of togetherness. So far, so good.

Took the family to the nearby Mead Wildlife Area today. Nature trails surrounding the Education Center and the Smoky Hill refuge entertained and educated all. Loons, cranes, swans, pelicans and waterfowl of many stripes were observed. What we failed to see was other families or nature lovers utilizing this public property. What a shame. The disconnect from the land remains a major issue as we struggle as a nation to put environmental troubles front and center.

Eighty years ago Aldo Leopold reminded us, "When we see land as a community to which we belong, we may begin to use it with love and respect - an extension of ethics. Perhaps such a shift of values can be achieved by reappraising things unnatural, tame, and confined in terms of things natural, wild, and free."

WHEN CRICKETS STOP CHIRPING

I sat in the shade of the alder clump,
near the hedgerow dividing our prairie,
when a turkey vulture suddenly appeared
drifting by with barely a wingbeat.
It covered the length of a forty in less than ten seconds.
Disappearing, I looked for another, but alas, he was a loner.

The cockers worked over the surrounding grassland,
hoping to roust a bird or two.
When they ran the length of the hedgerow, many small, unidentifiable
songbirds scattered left and right, disappearing
into the tall prairie grasses.
The wind was from the northwest -
cool, dry and carrying scents of autumn.
Sumac bursting scarlet red.
Swollen dogwood berries surrounded by bloodshot purple leaves.
All signs of seasonal change.

It was late August,
Hummingbirds and Orioles were staging and had begun migration.
Wildflowers were blooming in concert,
Black birds began to flock,
Nighthawks were swooping in from the north,
Velvet antlered white tailed bucks
had emerged from their summer hideouts,
and crickets were chirping for the last time.

Found myself alone at the homestead today. Our Maine bound family returned to their home on Tuesday. Everyone else retreated to a lake cottage near Wautoma. I'm home alone to tend the dogs and recuperate from a whirlwind week with my offspring - sons, daughter-in-laws, and four grandchildren. In a blink of an eye, our summer gathering has ended. All that's left is the memories. Wonderful memories.

Chores are done. Writing at my desk. Thinking about the cucumbers, zucchini delivered yesterday and the promise of surplus tomatoes from neighbor Kenny's garden. But what about sweet corn? We've had some, but the thought of honey dipped corn from Bancroft is bouncing in my head. Nothing is holding me in place here this afternoon, so dogs Buster and Finn will join me for a ride in the truck to the land of "Bucks, Birds and Berries". Then a drive through the Paul Olson prairie chicken and Meadow Valley wildlife areas will be a bonus!

August 28

At the closing bell of a cloudy wet weekend I observed a large hatch of dragonflies over our prairie field out back. Near the pond and over the hedgerow flew scores of these mosquito-eating flying "dragons". But what kind of dragonflies were they? A dragonfly is a dragonfly. Right? Since Wisconsin is home to 38 varieties, it's time to start learning the differences.

So we - the grandkids and I - set off on the Ranger to get pictures of our dragonflies for identification purposes. Easier said than done! Have you ever followed those flying demons and waited for them to pose for pictures?

I guess I'll need to heed Thoreau's recommendation;

"Happiness is like a butterfly, the more you chase it, the more it will evade you, but if you notice the other things around you, it will gently come and sit on your shoulder."

HERE IT COMES

From the west,
in short bursts at first,
mercury drops,
wind accelerates,
high clouds gather,
sun disappears,
humidity rises,
birds are silent,
and hiding in their copses,
hunters fidget,
gun dogs tremble,
here it comes,
fall arrives,
on a northwest storm-front.

September 1

Meteorology speaking, the first day of fall. Hunting wise, the first of a string of opening days. Later in the month the ruffed grouse season begins - in Wisconsin, always the Saturday closest to the 15th. Then, a week later, the northern half of the state opens to waterfowl hunting. Come October, the fall hunting seasons will all be underway.

Migrating swifts and nighthawks in September mark the beginning of autumn at our place along the creek. The season hunters have been waiting patiently for all year is finally here. Whether tagging along behind an upland bird dog, sitting by a cattail marsh, or perched high in a treestand - hunting for the devoted is much more than pulling a trigger or releasing an arrow.

For my non-hunting friends, keep in mind the famous conservationist Aldo Leopold, artist and poet, was an ardent hunter. His love and devotion for all things wild and free came from a lifetime of hunting and fishing in the outdoors.

Archived pictures show young Aldo, at three years of age, with a springer spaniel named Flick. A few years later, he followed the family dog into the woods carrying a single-shot shotgun and his father's words ringing in his ears, warning him against shooting birds from trees. Leopold wrote:

"My dog was good at treeing partridge and to forego a sure shot in the tree in favor of a hopeless one at the fleeing bird was my first exercise in ethical codes.... I could draw a map today of each clump of red bunchberry and each blue aster that adorned the mossy spot where he lay, my first partridge on the wing. I suspect my present affection for bunchberries and asters dates back to the day."

PEACE AND QUIET

*I've taken to sitting in my hunting blind during
the early morning hours at the end of our prairie
field now that the early seasons have begun.
Of note is the quietness surrounding this time of day.
A gentle breeze plucks at leaves and needles in the
surrounding woods. A car or truck may pass on the
adjacent gravel road, breaking the silence for a moment.
Geese may honk as they survey the river valley for
early harvested corn fields.*

*An occasional single engine plane flying in, or out of
Mosinee or Wausau or Stevens Point or a commercial
jet at 27,000 feet on its way to Minneapolis. As I
watched the latest of that kind, a flock of a dozen
Canada geese flew south overhead silently at
several hundred feet high. And dogs bark for
breakfast back at the kennels.*

September 9

No. 1 grandson, Wyatt, and I sat in our goose/dove blind this afternoon. He carried the same BB gun his father used when he was too young to carry a single shot shotgun. At six years old, what his attention span lacks is overridden by his enthusiasm. No shots were fired, but it was a grand time nonetheless.

September 11

55 degrees, cloudy and a light breeze is from the northwest. Perfect sitting weather out back over geese and dove decoys. Put on my rubber bottom boots to keep my socks dry after yester-

31

day's one inch rainfall. A few lingering migrant nighthawks. A couple of high flying southbound flocks of Canada geese, not interested in me, my goose call and decoys. Several doves, past by out of range - and like the geese, not interested my artificial doves placed over the food plot.

September 15

No. 3 grandson, Rykar, and I inspected the goose silhouette decoys I had placed on the mowed food plot today. He had to "touch" all five and tried to reset the one that had fallen over in the wind. At 2, going on 3, he had all he could do to push the decoy's stake into the hard packed soil. Once he was satisfied he climbed aboard the UTV and continued our ride around the prairie grass field. But not before Papa let him blow on the goose call hanging from the rear view mirror. Not much pleases him more than to blow that call for all the world to hear. Except maybe one of his Nina's snack bags!

GETTING OLDER

After more than 50 years of collecting worldly possessions, I've been told by my family it's time to downsize. Time has found me in an office and kennel, two hundred feet from our 100-year old house in the country. An outbuilding built especially for my dogs and me in retirement. Now, after ten years, the office, kennel and attached garage is chuck full of lifetime memories. I knew this time would come. I must have, because six years ago I wrote the following column for my weekly outdoor newspaper column;

"For lack of a better term, I'll simply call them things. You know, objects of great importance that one saves for pure personal reasons. For this old hunter, my collection of things is getting out of hand. Guns,

knives, books, magazines, decoys, dog collars, hats, hunting vests and coats, framed pictures, photos, mounted deer heads and game birds, old calendars, old shell boxes, dog whistles and bells, and duck and goose calls. The boss affectionately refers to my things as junk. To that end, when I retired three years ago, we moved my things to a new kennel office – built large enough to house my treasured possessions.

Here I sit at my writing desk, surrounded by things that bring me great comfort. Hundreds of books and magazines at my fingertips – some I may never get around to reading. Three gun cabinets housing more guns than a man needs - and as we speak, I search for another vintage double barreled shotgun that's been on my bucket list for years. "What will that gun do that your other ones are incapable of doing?" the boss inquired. "Remember, my car needs new brakes."

My old duck decoy collection numbers 17. I lost track of the number of newer ones - stored elsewhere in the kennel. Oh, and the half dozen stashed in the blind down by our pond. And hunting clothes - vests, coats and hats - hanging throughout the building. Who doesn't need a good assortment of hats? Blaze orange ones, camouflaged ones and all other colors of the spectrum. Nearly 40 framed pictures, plates and plaques decorate the office walls. Select images of favorite bird dogs from 42 years of ownership. A modest assembly of trophies and ribbons earned by them are on display - collecting dust just as well as several trophy deer heads and mounted gamebirds. And No. 2 son's trophy largemouth bass.

Antlers from over the decades. My first buck – a fork horn shot in the Chequamegon national forest. My two boys' first bucks. Others, too many for the office walls, are displayed alongside posters, fishing poles and license plates on the walls of the adjacent cluttered workshop.

Back in the office are a hodge-podge of tail feathers. Buster, my side-kick cocker spaniel's first grouse tail feathers. No. 1 son's first turkey fan *and a woodcock. Sharptail, Hun and pheasant tail feathers from the past and several protruding out of a spent shotgun shell from the latest trip west.*

Turkey, predator, deer calls and of course, an assortment of duck calls take residence in my office. I never mastered the highball call of a mallard, but could chuckle a feeding melody with the best of them. And if I could have a dollar for every goose I made turn its head over the years, well, a new used old gun and brakes would be in order. Among the calls in my possession is a treasured one that took on new meaning last week when this paper announced the untimely death of Byron Herbert Shaw, professor emeritus at our local university. Bill Berry described Shaw as a nationally recognized trailblazing expert in water resources and went on to note, 'he was also a wine-maker, a friend to hundreds, a wood-worker, farmer, canoeist, camper, hunter, and traveler.' I knew Byron on campus back in the 70s, later professionally in the world of water resources and finally as a wood-worker. Several years ago while drooling over one of his handmade wooden canoes, I bought one of his handcrafted goose calls. This work of art remains one of my favorites and will forever bring its maker to mind when I use it or spy it on display.

An old hunter must prepare for the inevitable. A time when the body wears out and moments afield have diminished. A time when a good book will transport his weary body back to the sweet alder, aspen and dogwood coverts – to the potholes and prairie grasslands he once knew so well. A time when his favorite double gun will only go as far as his lap and recliner – where he'll run an oily rag up and down the barrel, caress the walnut stock, dream of the past and smile.

Until then, this old hunter will continue to collect things made for lasting memories."

Today, six-years later, I sit at my writing desk as my wonderful daughter-in-law, bless her heart, slaves away deep cleaning the attached dog kennel. Already, she has cleaned out much of the excess stuff. Dusty dog training equipment hanging on one of two wall peg boards will be sorted, stored or sold. The old golf club driver, resting on one peg board that they laughed at and said, "Must go!" was a memory from a brief run on my high school golf team. Of late, it has served to open pocket windows out of reach on the wall over kennel runs. Soon, she and No. 2 son will begin the process of bringing a dozen or more plastic totes full of "things" into my office - one at a time. There, I will decide what must stay and what must go. Oh boy.

One of my favorite outdoor writers, the late Gene Hill wrote, "I am almost through my life and no one has ever asked me what I felt about the lunge of a bass, the flush of a grouse or the sudden appearance of a deer. No one will ever know, but you, how much I still miss my dogs that died. Or how hard I wish for the dream to live a special day or so all over again. Or how much I like to be alone. They don't understand why I have lined a wall with guns that I almost never use. Why I save old boots and hats and hunting clothes. They don't understand that what is just an old coat is a memory to me. They see a man who is getting old… surrounded by old things. A worn-out-man. . . wearing worn-out boots and covered by a worn-out coat."

September 17

Opening day of the 2022 ruffed grouse season. After a morning of chores and checking in 4 boarding dogs at the kennel, I made my way northeast to some county-owned land called Leathercamp. The truck thermometer read 79 degrees by the time I reached my destination, making it a good day to scout from the road in air conditioned bliss. The lack of other vehicles, save a bow hunter's or two, was a true indicator that it was too hot by mid-day to safely run bird dogs.

So we headed west, Buster (riding shotgun) and me, to the state-owned Mead Wildlife Area. That too became a rideabout with the same result. The only other bird hunters I saw were standing outside a local bar/diner in their blaze orange hunting gear. The waterfowl refuge was loaded with pre-season ducks and geese near Smokey Hill, while the gravel roads and parking areas bordering great upland grouse and woodcock cover were void of any hunting activity.

Seems the majority are waiting for more cool, fall-like weather to officially open the season. Perhaps rulemakers need to rethink this mid-September opener.

September 19

My logger stopped by and mowed the trail surrounding a 5-acre woodlot planned for cutting and an adjacent log landing area. Soon he'll return and begin the process of clear cutting those acres of maturing aspen, maple and basswood. Just south of the marsh that drains excess water from the west and north - where I created a trail after the previous landowner logged off all trees 8 inches or larger in diameter in 1984.

This clearcut will resprout in aspen and in a few years harbor thousands of young saplings, so thick as to prevent anyone from walking through. Immediately, deer will browse on the leftover tops and come next spring, woodcock will skydance and nest on the open forest floor. In time, and with luck, ruffed grouse will occupy this section of our woods and perhaps a male will drum for a mate or two from a nearby drumming log.

September 22

The autumnal equinox—also called the September equinox or fall equinox—arrived today. This day marks the beginning of fall in the Northern Hemisphere and spring in the Southern

Hemisphere. The northwest winds of autumn arrived yesterday when daytime temperatures dropped 20 degrees to the 30s and 40s overnight. Color changes to deciduous foliage have appeared - scattered here and there on the leaves of many sumac, dogwood, birch and alder. Large flocks of blackbirds are gathering in the cattails and treetops. Geese and cranes are restless, joining eagles, hawks and vultures while testing updrafts. Several were spotted above the clouds, circling in the jet streams, then diving back to lower heights above the treetops. Not quite ready to head south. Not yet.

> *"The woods are lovely, dark and deep. But I have promises to keep,*
> *and miles to go before I sleep."*
> *~Robert Frost*

September 23

Picked up some apples this week in SW Wisconsin's Driftless hills. Not just any apples, but Bailey Sweets, an apple outdoor writer Gordon MacQuarrie made famous in his Milwaukee Journal newspaper column and books. On his way north in autumn, he'd stop at a farmer's roadside produce stand and buy a bag. Mac's favorite apple variety, he'd note a couple in his pockets, was just the ticket while hunting partridge in October.

We bought 5 1/2 pecks yesterday. I told the apple orchard guy about MacQuarrie. He chased us down as we loaded the truck and handed us another 1/2 peck, thinking we wouldn't mind a few more! 3 pecks seemed just about right!

September 24

Opening day of woodcock season 2022. Yep, lots of memories- all the way back to the fall of 1972 when four college buddies using pumps and automatic 12 gauges hunting Mike's "40" on the Buena Vista Marsh. This time, our 50th consecutive year, I met friend Dale just south and west of Mike's place on a small piece of prairie chicken state land where we band woodcock on their singing grounds each spring. Unfortunately, three members of our traditional group are at their 94 year-old father's hospital bedside. Damn Covid. We hunted Dale's German Wirehaired Griffon, Dexter. 12-year-old Buster was left in his kennel box, as I'm not ready to turn him loose in the woods -as his hearing is so bad, I'm afraid he'll lose track of me. A GPS tracker collar will go into use soon.

We moved 4 birds. Dexter pointed 2. Yours truly missed one of those 2.

WHEN?

I stare up at the moon and stars and ask who?
I pause and wonder what?
Then follow up with when and where and why?
Some people stop at who?
Others finish at what?
The rest may end with when, where and why?
My dog seldom, if ever, looks up at the heavens,
unless he's scanning the horizon for incoming
ducks, geese or doves.
He only wonders when?

September 26

After several unproductive days in our back 40 goose/dove blind, timely news arrived today about next month's grouse camp. Optimism runs high as we plan on this annual trip up to northwestern Wisconsin. Tim Wilder wrote this morning, "As of now I am planning to be at Grouse Camp 8-11 October." But until then, I'll hunt closer to home and venture to Tim's backyard at Fort McCoy where we'll hunt grouse and woodcock for what has become another annual event.

REMINISCING ON BIRDDOGS

My dog knows better than me, the way
to the quarry we seek. He follows his
nose, ten-thousand fold greater than
mine, along a scent cone leading to
feathers covering the king or prince
of upland game birds - ruffed grouse
or woodcock?

To the dog, facing the wind, the scent
tells the story. Which way did it go?
How long ago? What species of bird?
How close is it now? Then the moment of truth.

The pointing dog stands rock solid.
Trembling, oh so slightly. Nostrils flaring.
Eyes and head cocked gently sideways,
as to catch a glimpse of me, approaching
from the side to push the hidden bird to flight.

Or the flushing dog. At close range, tail
wagging furiously. Cutting back and forth
through the cone. Scent droplets hanging
in the air and spread on ground level vegetation.
Then nearing its quarry, slows to prepare for
one last push and flush. An explosion of bird
and dog, both gone air bound.

I've followed dogs of both stripes. So many
over the years I've lost count. But the end
result has remained the same. Bird at the
end of the scent cone. Walk in for the flush,
or let the flushing dog do the job.

A hit or a miss. A bird or two in the bag.
Smothered in onions, mushrooms and
creamy gravy - a meal meant for kings,
queens and rough shooting hunters.

September 29

Tested positive for Covid today. That explains the recent cough, fever and cold. Doctor prescribed Paxlovid and hopefully, I should be better in a day or two.

TOO OLD TO DIE YOUNG

I'm too old to die young.
It's been said, only the good die young.
Guess I wasn't good enough.
Now, I'm too old to die young.
They say only the elderly are subject to pandemics.
The young and others seem oblivious,
As they flock to crowded bars, restaurants, pools,
protests, rallies and other social gatherings.
All without masks.
Meanwhile, politicians seem content to play
Russian roulette with our children, teachers, health
care workers, and struggling small businesses.
Maybe I'm too old to die young.

October 1

October. The best time of the year. Waiting for this month all year long is a burden we must bear - if only to enjoy the fruits of the tenth month. Frosty mornings, changing colors of the leaves, mass migration of birds heading south, duck blinds, deer stands, logging roads and light snow flurries.

And I'm over covid - the doctor was right.

OCTOBER

Who among us can gaze across the landscape
at this moment in time without wonder?
What power - beyond the science of it all - creates
the brilliant shades of yellow, orange, and red?
We know the green pigment in leaves is chlorophyll
and thrives only in warm weather. As temperatures
drop and daylight hours diminish, carotene and
anthocyanin pigments persist and cause leaves
to appear yellow and red respectively. Picture postcard
beauty beyond description lies in view and can
soften even the hardest of hearts.
I dare to ponder - who really controls the paintbrush?

October 4

Drove to Colby to pick up 20 bobwhite quail from a fellow who raises a few hundred each year in his barn. At $10 a piece, it's what one would expect to pay this time of year. Chicks are much cheaper, young flyers maybe $6, but "flight ready" adults in the fall demand top dollar. A call to the Wolf River Game Farm, where I've purchased birds in the past, revealed all birds were spoken for - as game farm hunters pay a premium to hunt them in the fall. Our 20 went right into the johnny house we maintain on the edge of our prairie field out back. Oh boy, the cockers are in for a training treat this fall!

October 7

Hooked up the large trailer to the truck and headed to Neceedah, to drop off a pair of boarding cockers and where a used golf cart awaited our possession. Longtime client and artist Dale Steele had generously given her cart to us to use around our property. She recently upgraded to a John Deere Gator and when she learned the boss wanted a cart to transport the grandkids around our mowed trails, she eagerly insisted we take her electric golf cart. Since her longstanding business was sure to continue, we made a deal to exchange the cart's value in future boarding bills.

October 12

Grouse Camp 2022. Departed to the northwest and the Saint Croix/Gordon area. Wall tents set by friend Rich. Arrived and greeted by three old friends and one new one - Bill, a former deer biologist with the DNR who now lives on a farm in Montana. He also owns an inherited farm in Australia where he was born. Another story for another time. The campfire stories were priceless, as were the stories from our good friends from Georgia - Darron and Buddy Ray.

"Nature always wears the colors of the spirit."
~Ralph Waldo Emerson

October 13

A day spent hunting grouse and woodcock and ducks. My quest was to locate a spring lake in the Douglas County forest, a mile back on a logging road - a favorite of famous newspaper outdoor writer Gordon MacQuarrie back in the 1930s and 40s. Mission accomplished. Sat on the shores of the lake with my sidekick Buster and watched several flocks of diving ducks land out of range and a pair of bald eagles soaring overhead. Sipped coffee, ate Bailey Sweet apples (see September 23rd entry) and meditated for a couple of hours. It was glorious!

Then traveled northeast to the Namekagon Barrens, where I explored, took pictures and looked for sharptail grouse. This was how the landscape looked after early loggers cut over the northwoods at the turn of the century - and sharptails and prairie chicken ruled northern Wisconsin.

October 14

Bid farewell to my camp buddies and headed to Pastor Craig's place in Ladysmith. But not before meeting up with Kieth Crowley, MacQuarrie biographer and national award winning photographer extraordinaire in Hayward. I exchanged a half peck of Bailey Sweet apples for a jar of Keith's wife's wild raspberry jam. We both shared MacQuarrie stories and current hunting tales. He and his wife were closing on a new home in Arizona, where he and his setter will soon be chasing desert quail during the dead of winter. His home on Middle eau Claire Lake will be awaiting their return next spring. Always a great visit with Keith.

October 15

A youth and adult mentoring grouse and woodcock biology and hunting clinic north of Hawkins today. Pastor Craig invited me to participate and share my knowledge on woodcock banding, hunting and hunting dogs. It was show and tell with my field bred English Cockers Buster and Mitzie and Craig's German shorthair, Millie. Was a very enjoyable day off the grid in the Flambeau River State Forest.

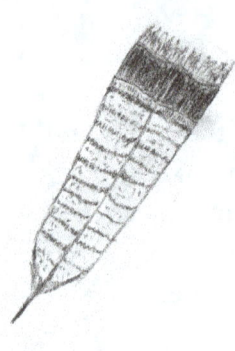

BLOWING IN THE WIND

Why, oh why do some
birds fly so high,
while others barely
clear the tree line?
And why do some fly
alone, while others
travel in scattered flocks?

Geese and ducks fly
in formal formation.
Hawks and vultures drift
south while circling windward.
Cranes spiral high, hoping
to catch upper air streams
and drift southbound with ease.
Crows fly in murders, looking
for evening roosts, roadkills,
or owls and hawks to harass.
Blackbirds flock in mass come
fall - sharing time with corn-
fields and cattails.

Birds would rather fly than
walk, lest becoming a pile
of feathers.

Annual end of the camping season when son Karl and I took the camper to the nearby Dubay County Park's RV dump station. Only two campers in the park as the official closing will be on October 31st. Parking the camper for the winter is bittersweet, but its presence covered in snow in the backyard promises warmer weather down the line.

Kids are here and it'll be time for running the cockers on quail released from the johnny house (see October 4th entry). Cockers Raven and Mitzie are getting the most use of these training birds. Once half the flock are released and scattered during the training process, they eventually return before dark into a funnel designed to let them back into the house where their food, water and cousins await.

A WORLD FAMOUS BIRD HUNTER

The year was 1899. A young boy of twelve followed his father Carl hunting along the Mississippi River. Carl was a hunter of great local reputation - during the days of year-round market hunting – with a well-developed personal code of sportsmanship. No spring waterfowl hunting for this sportsman. He never hunted after the sun went down. He set his own personal bag limits when there were none. Rand' s father taught him well and started him with a single barreled shotgun. Gun safety was paramount; "Never point a gun at anything you don't intend to kill."

In 1945 Rand, now a seasoned hunter and writer, vividly recalled shooting his first ruffed grouse. That " partridge" came after nearly two unsuccessful seasons behind his dog. The dog often treed partridge, but his father' s words echoed in his head. " You may not shoot partridge from trees. You're old enough to learn wing-shooting."

"A big partridge rose with a roar at my left...crossed behind me hell-bent for the nearest cedar swamp ...a swinging shot ...and the bird tumbled dead in a shower of feathers and golden leaves."

Ethical lessons learned well indeed. Young Rand Aldo Leopold later became quite famous, and today he is universally remembered simply as Aldo Leopold.

Leopold wore many hats – forester, botanist, wildlife manager, writer, poet, philosopher, professor – but by all accounts, he was first and foremost a hunter. From childhood to the end of his life he followed his family's faithful gun dogs. Many of his firsthand nature lessons were learned afield with his German Shorthaired Pointer (GSP) "Gus," and inspired many of the essays found in his classic "A Sand County Almanac."

From his base camp "shack" along the Wisconsin River in Sauk County, he and Gus hunted grouse, woodcock, pheasant and quail. His extremely detailed hunting journals chronicled those hunts during the 1920s until his untimely death in 1948.

October 30

Whitetail bucks are now in rut. Counted a half dozen of their "scrapes" on the ground and that again many "rubs" on tree trunks. Attracting female deer in season and warning other bucks intruding their home range is the name of the game these days. The first week in November is traditionally the peak of the rut. Look out motorists! When bucks start chasing the does, travel on roadways becomes treacherous. Just ask daughter-in-law Meghan. She clobbered one with her van late last week.

On the eve of November, unseasonably warm weather greet Halloween trick or treaters. 60 to 70 degree days into the new month is highly unusual. Seems to have put the brakes on migrating birds, as woodcock continue to trickle through central Wisconsin. This Wednesday, friend Dale and I will hunt on the Buena Vista. I will use my DNR issued permit to access territory I haven't seen for years on my Polaris Ranger.

Sat out back with Buster when the geese started flying this morning. While waiting for the next flock to pass by I called my friend Ron Hvizdak in Montana to tell him the sad news about Glen Rutz's passing. His son Mike, Ron and I were the 3 musketeers in high school and Glen was a big part of our lives back then.

SEASON'S ENDING
Now that our seasons and trails are closer to the end
than the beginning.
I enjoy a slower pace, closer working bird dogs, smelling
the roses and logging roads.
A nap against a tree, scratching the dog's head resting on a
knee is all I need. Just being there is now the name
of the game.

November means many things to many people. For those of us that live north of the tension zone, it represents a transition from warm weather to cold – from daylight savings to standard time – from rainbow colors to drab. However, to the hunter, November - despite the changes - remains food for the soul.

The neighbor's corn picker arrived yesterday. After doing some maintenance, the operator made one pass and parked the rig for the night. I'll be watching the picking progress closely over the next few days. Freshly harvested fields could attract geese, ducks and doves. And I'll be waiting in ambush on the corner of our adjacent 5 acre cheese factory woods with decoys. Stay tuned.

With two days of rain in the forecast, it looks like Sunday and Monday, the last two days of this year's woodcock season will have to work for Mike, Dale and me to end the hunt on the Buena Vista marsh together. Up to 2 or more inches are predicted by Saturday night. We can use the precipitation, as Vera's Pond is going into the freeze up as low as I can remember.

THE FINAL RUN

On Sunday, he hunted woodcock for an hour with us one last time. On Monday, the last day of the season, he remained in the truck while we hunted with his daughter. He took one last lap - the final run around our field by the creek that evening. He collapsed from exhaustion 100 yards from the house. We rested for a while and he climbed the front stairs of the house. On Tuesday evening, he napped on my lap one last time. He fell asleep forever on the floor by my side an hour later. My friend and constant companion for the past twelve and a half years, Buster, is gone. Please don't despair, but join me in celebrating his twelve trips around the sun.

From the day we brought him home from Schroeder's Fallen

Wings Kennel, my wife and I knew we had one special dog. She cuddled him in her lap and declared English Cockers were perfect lap dogs compared to our kennel full of sixty-pound German Shorthairs. That fall he traveled with me to Saskatchewan, followed by many years to North Dakota, northern Wisconsin grouse camps and of course just about everywhere else in our home state. Over the years woodcock, ruffed grouse, Hungarian partridge, pheasants, sharptail grouse, quail, ducks and geese all met their match in Buster. I'll never forget the time he dove underwater to retrieve a wounded wood duck.

His exploits over the years gained him a bit of notoriety in my weekly outdoor newspaper column and entries on my kennel's Facebook account. He even earned a chapter in my book, Wisconsin Bird Hunting Tales. He graces a page or two in Kieth Crowley's book Pheasant Dogs. And he became the inspiration for a novel I am currently working on entitled Chequamegon, Moon River - a northern Wisconsin murder mystery. It's a story of a boy, his cocker spaniel dog, coming of age and falling in love.

Over the years, Buster sired over sixty pups, much to the delight of over sixty new owners. His offspring made their way as far as Alaska, Tennessee, Georgia, Minnesota, Indiana, Illinois, Michigan, South Dakota and Nebraska. Much to my delight and comfort, three of Buster's daughters remain with us and God willing, two will carry his bloodline into the future.

I buried Buster yesterday down by the creek. Under the shadow of a pair of walnut trees that sprung up from seeds I planted years ago. Near a "johnny house" that currently houses 19 bobwhite quail - that sing every day for others of their kind released in the training field. Buried next to our cocker Belle, who passed last year. And a stone's throw from the creek that bisects our forty acres.

When I die in my 99th year, I will have left instructions for my family to spread my ashes over Buster's grave. It'll be a fine place to spend eternity with my friend and constant companion, Buster - on the final run.

November 11

A thirty degree drop in temperature overnight has turned the table on the fall season. Extended high temperatures in the thirties. Snow flurries are in the forecast and 3-5 inches predicted for the Upper Peninsula today. Put away the hoses and put the plow on the Ranger. Mister Heater is in my deer blind along the creek and the countdown to the deer rifle season is on. In the meantime, the rut is still on. Time to sit with my crossbow in the blind. Let it snow!

November 12

The countdown begins. 7 days until the opening of this year's 9-day deer hunt. A time when over a half million hunters hit the woods and occupy their stands across the state. Come daylight, the highly anticipated event will come to pass. Pastor Craig and his son Josh, nephew Paul and his son Quinn and I will take our regular positions along the creek and trails. My new deer blind mentioned yesterday should suit me well.

November 14

Looks like we're into an extended cold snap. With highs only in the upper 20s, low 30s, going into the opening weekend of the deer hunt, it's time to get out the cold weather gear and check out the Mr. Heater for my deer blind. I may turn out the quail flock this week and let them fend for themselves. The water dish in the Johnny House remains frozen. Repositioning an old Pheasant Forever ground feeder nearby may be in order. The cover across the prairie field remains tall and strong and should afford them protection from predators and the cold. Water from the creek and pond is still at hand.

MY OLD TRUCK

She'd been around so long I couldn't find her title of certification. Nearly twenty years old, with over 200,000 miles, she'd seen better days. Nickel and dimed me to death of late. She was reliable within an hour of home. Untrustworthy beyond that. It was time. Time to replace an old truck once again.

Since college days, I've only owned pickups. Lots of them. Ten to be exact. The family station wagons I inherited before trucks were merely transportation. Vehicles prone to getting stuck. My lifestyle required the services of a workhorse. Trucks would fit the bill. Four wheel drive became imperative. Hauling multiple dogs called for multiple dog boxes. My first truck carried a homemade wooden 3-hole box. And with the gear required to hunt and fish across Wisconsin's northwoods, a vehicle like a pickup was my only choice.

Today's retiring old truck took me west multiple times. Several times to the Dakotas after pheasants, sharp tailed grouse, Hungarian partridge and waterfowl. Two extended trips to the Saskatchewan prairies. A workhorse indeed. No mechanical issues to speak of. But as of late, and after 200,000 miles, she's showing her age. The old black truck just ain't what she used to be.

At sixty-six years old, I was in need of another truck. Except for a Jeep Comanche pickup back in the late 1980s, my brand of choice has always been Ford. My first, used 1968 was called a F-100 Custom. Then in 1979, I bought a new F-150 off a dealer's lot in Wausau. Forty-one years later, a 2019 version has come home to our roost. Life expectancy for both of us, my new truck and me, means this ought to be my last.

And therein lies the reason for this rambling. This outdoorsman's truck is an extension of his being. A brand new truck is but a new beginning. The four large totes of "stuff" taken out of the old black truck sit in the garage right now, ready to be carefully sorted and organized for the new black truck. Bound and determined to do a better job of keeping my new rig neater, I've obtained a slide-out drawer organizer - which will hold all the fishing and hunting gear in the bed of the truck. On top of that will ride a recycled 3-hole aluminum dog box. Covering it all, will rest a black Fiberglass topper with side opening windows.

You get the picture. I'm attempting to put together the ideal traveling old man's sportsman truck. Time's a wastin. Soon I'll need to be organized and ready to go at a moment's notice.

November 18

The gang's rolling in for this year's deer season, with the Zandi boys arriving first. Pastor Craig and wife Janice came first this afternoon and he and I checked stands and put Mr. Heater in my elevated stand on the northeast corner of our 5-acre woodlot across the road from the kennel and house. Their son Josh arrived after dark and settled in the house. The weather forecast is for 7 degrees at daybreak.

SOUND OF BELLS

I love the
potpourri of
autumn smells.
The odor of
decomposing
aspen leaves,
rotting pine needles,
marsh alder and
cattail muck,
wet gun dogs,
gunpowder drifting
in the air, gun oil
and Hoppe's No. 9.

I love the memory of
October portraits.
Smoky gold tamaracks,
shades of yellow aspen,
scarlet red and brilliant
orange maples, dark
green pines and chocolate
brown oak leaves.

The touch of the season.
I relish the texture of
leather gloves,
nylon chaps,
rubber bottom boots,
walnut gunstocks,
wet dogs, and frost
numbed fingertips.

The sounds of autumn
echoing in my mind.
Trumpeting cranes,
Honking geese,
Highballing mallards,
The twitter of flushing woodcock,
Cackling rooster pheasants,
Thundering ruffed grouse,
And the sound of bells -
bird dog bells.

November 19

Opening day of the 2022 deer hunting season. Nephew Paul, grandnephew Quinn, and grandniece Josey arrived before daybreak. From our frigid stands we saw plenty of does and fawns, but only 3 bucks. Pastor Craig missed a six-pointer when a tree intercepted his bullet. I saw 5 does and fawns early in the morning, but nothing in the afternoon. A flock of 19 turkeys entertained me while feeding in the partially picked cornfield that surrounded my deer stand. Craig and his wife left for home in Ladysmith after supper - in order to perform Sunday worship services.

November 20

Day 2. Not much warmer in the morning, but moderated in the afternoon. Our luck turned at the end of the day when Josh tagged a very nice 9-pointer. I saw 3 deer escaping our 5-acre woodlot behind my stand fifteen minutes before closing time. A doe and two fawns. Retrieved Josh's buck with my Ranger, hung it in the garage and he had it skinned and quartered before we ate supper. Another Zandi tradition - speed deer processing.

Day 3. Josh headed home this morning after taking his deer carcass to the DNR's dumping station at the Mead Wildlife Area headquarters. I went into hunt-at-will status, now being alone. Funny how my drive lessens when deer camp companions disappear.

ALL IT TOOK

Was the sight of two deer running
across the field near my stand.
To lure me from kennel chores
and the warmth of my office.
To an empty deer stand.

It was the seventh day
of the pandemic deer hunt.
Day six found me laid up
after a painful twist of fate
and my right leg.
A tumble in the dark while
feeding the wood-stove on
Thanksgiving eve cast the spell.
Remedy came from painkilling
pills and ice packs.

Our three hunters took three deer
over the first weekend,
but I still had a buck tag to fill.
The flock of swans that rested
several days on nearby Dubay
flew over my stand today on their way
southeast to Chesapeake.

*I pity those that have never
cherished the warmth
and comfort sunshine affords a
face early on frigid
mornings in a deer, duck or
turkey blind.*

*I feel for those that have
missed the soul cleansing
effect received by hours spent
alone in that manner. And for
the chosen, the love and
companionship a wife and
parcel of hunting dogs
provides is immeasurable. I
thank my lucky stars - I've
had a lifetime of all of that.*

November 22

Country living has its ups and downs. Mostly ups, but occasionally things turn sour. Like when you experience what I call "septic woes". Imagine not being able to flush your toilets and the household drains back up. And on a weekend when plumber's rates double. Well, it happened after our deer hunting friends left and the grandchildren and their parents weren't visiting. So, we - the boss and I - had time to unplug the inlet pipe to the septic tank. This was the second time we tackled the problem, so we knew what to do. After much plunging and checking the pumping chamber, we dug up and popped the tank's cement cover, revealing the problem plug. Sparing you the gorey details, we successfully fixed the problem - and presto, all drains flowed just fine. Not bad for a couple of senior citizens!

Day 8. Bless his heart, Quinn came back to deer camp for the last weekend. We both resumed our early season stands. While we didn't see any deer and the surrounding township was mostly quiet, we did enjoy warmer weather.

December 1

The ponds have frozen over. The ground is white from late November and early December snowfalls. Winter is officially here. The grandkids visit and put a new perspective to an old person's view of the coldest time of the year. Here's a few questions from our youngest grandchild, Rykar.

WHAT HAPPENED TO WATER?

Taking things for granted
becomes the norm
the older we get.
Like ponds freezing over.
Plants dying from the cold.
Rain changing to snow.
But today, our two year old
grandson gave us pause
to ponder. He asked,
"Where water go?"

while walking on the frozen pond
and picking cattails.
"Where peppers go?"
while filling bird-feeders with
grandma and passing by the
raised vegetable beds.
Elders reflect as toddlers discover.
Together we rejoice in nature's ways.

December 3

Snowflakes in December, when put under a microscope, bring the world of art and science into concert - and draw the observer into another dimension. In 1880, fifteen-year-old Vermont farmer Wilson Bentley, drew pictures of his "tiny miracles of beauty" and by age twenty, devised a method to catch flakes on a velvet cloth and photograph their image before they melted. Over his lifetime, he recorded over 5,000 different ice crystal shapes - no two alike!

WINTER WINDS

Seasonal winds carry different voices.
Singing the promise of spring,
Blowing gentle melodies in summer,
Crackling and snapping come fall,
Howling menacing forecasts in winter.

I let the dog outside the other evening
to the sound of winter winds blowing
through the stand of white pines

along the edge of the old line fence.
Howling menacing best described it's
voice that early frigid December night.
It was then I contemplated various
voices winds present to human ears.

Different when passing across a sea
of grassland. Altogether a separate voice
when roaring through the upper branches
of fifty-foot white pines - or independent
from red pine articulations. Wind blowing
through winter's copper colored oak leaves,
hanging on for dear life, sound much
unlike wind whisking along acres
of a bare branched aspen clearcut.
So, stand with me amid a winter
windblown stand of anything and
let us guess. Are winter winds defined
by the company they keep, the speed
which they travel, or the interpretation
of the beholder?

December 5

The ponds on our property number three. The "Original Pond" was created when the previous owner, a well-meaning, but poor farmer had a road plowed through the woods from one field to another - two hundred yards to the north. Without regard to the wetlands, and before enforceable regulations, a bulldozer backed up the natural drainage of the woods. As the water backed up, a pond resulted, with excess runoff trickling over the new farm lane. After we took ownership at a Sheriff auction, an Army Corp of Engineering agent told me the pond and farm lane could stay and that I could upgrade the lane as needed.

"Vera's Pond" was created when we traded a used red Chevette to our neighbor Dave, whose father owned and operated a rather large bulldozer. Cliff was in charge of scraping out a low spot in the field east of the house and kennel. Also approved by the agent and permitted by the county, the resulting pond has proven worth its weight in gold over the years as a dog training, tadpole and frog hunting hotspot, and waterfowl stopover.

A second bulldozed pond lies deeper in the woods. Dubbed "Golden Pond" by its creator Cliff, it gained its name when he left a hand painted sign of the same name on its banks when he finished. This isolated pond is the deepest and well-fed of the three that retains a decent water level even in the driest of years.

All 3 are frozen solid now and support the antics of exploring critters and grandkids.

December 6

Blackbirds were plentiful along the creek this past summer. This fall large flocks congregated over the cornfield across the gravel road. At night they roosted in the cattails on one of our ponds. During the summer months they nested in the same cattails.

Leave it to the grandkids to find the nests when the pond freezes over. Last week, the kids set a record by finding 6 nests. The experts say each female produces 2-4 eggs and up to 2 clutches per year. So, our pond's 6 nests potentially produced 24 - 48 more blackbirds this year.

Perhaps that's why flocks of blackbirds are so large come October! But it's December and our flock is now somewhere south of the Mason-Dixon line.

December 10

A drive-about of nearby 33,000 acre Mead Wildlife Area to grouse hunt was unfruitful. It was the third day of a special state-wide whitetail doe season with only small interest by blaze orange clad hunters. I observed scores of ice fishermen on Dubay and Big Eau Pleine reservoirs, but only a handful of hunters. This is the season for fishermen when fabled "first ice" allows the faithful a return to frozen water they enjoy during the coldest time of the year.

December 11

A Raven flew by and called out from the woods and behind the kennel this morning. It sounded like a hen turkey's gurgled cluck, so much so, that I quickly scanned the woods behind the kennel exercise area for the local flock on their morning stroll. But then, I spied the Raven flying low over the treetops heading northwest. Experts describe this Raven call as a liquidly water droplet sound - and indeed recordings of that particulate call does resemble a hen turkey's gurgled clucking. Watch, listen and learn.

December 14

A predicted winter storm arrived last night in the form of ice and sleet, followed by freezing rain. This, the weatherman says, will be followed by up to 10 inches of snow tonight. No school for the grandkids for up to 2 days. And by Friday, it will taper off to flurries. That's good news, as I need to drive east to Green Bay in the morning for a scheduled vet appointment to have Mitzie's and Raven's hips x-rayed for OFA certification.

THE WOLF TREE

They're called wolf trees.
Too big to knock over,
spared the plow,
and in the way when
a farmer cleared the land.
Ours is bent, a sign of
it's struggle with a dozer fifty
years ago.

Once bordering the edge of a
cornfield, it survives sheltered
from the sun, as pine, popple and
alder creep into the now dormant
cropland turned prairie grassland.
Our wolf tree reminds us of
days gone by and a special bird dog
named Tina.

Tina was buried under the wolf tree thirty-
some years ago. Today, her picture hangs on
my office wall. She was a second generation
German Shorthaired Pointer, an early reminder
of a fifty-year old breeding program.
Many other shorthairs have come and gone
and while they all share space in my

memory bank, only a select few rise to the
top of the list. Tina was one of those.

So, when passing the wolf tree these days I
smile, stop and say hi.
Then withdraw a few fond memories from
the bank.

December 16

Another snowfall of about 3 inches this morning resulted in slippery roads. Not the best day to undertake a road trip to Green Bay. But a scheduled veterinarian appointment with Doc Alan Dunbar could not wait. Two of our cockers needed x-rays for OFA certification. Both Raven and Mitzi are ready for breeding later this winter and hip certification is important for breed health going forward. And, for Raven's stud qualifications for other potential mates in the future.

Anywho…I hadn't seen Alan for twenty-some years, and that in itself was worth the 2-hour precarious drive. We had time to chat and reminisce a bit and plan for a visit to his kennel and horse farm in the Oconto County countryside next spring.

December 19

The Consolidated Water & Power Company maintains the nearby Dubay Dam and Lake Dubay Reservoir. Along with that, a 30-mile high-powered electrical transmission line that happens to turn west in our front yard by way of a giant western pine power pole planted on our corner of County Roads E & H. On this day a CW&PC worker turned his pickup around in our kennel driveway and proceeded to slip into the deep road ditch.

I came to the young man's rescue by offering to help pull him out with my truck and tow strap. Only succeeded in spinning tires, so I fired up our John Deere tractor. With much tugging and spinning of tires, out came their truck and they were able to make their appointment in Wisconsin Rapids by noon.

December 20

The Towers. The Mid State Poets Tower (MSPT), a writers group to which I belong, had a monthly meeting tonight. The annual Xmas meeting. I brought a crockpot full of Lynda's Swedish meatballs and came home with a pint of Isherwood pure maple syrup. "Senator" Lawlor gave me a lead on Percy Bysshe Shelley's "Ode to the West Wind" after I read my essays "Blowing in the Wind" and "Winter Winds".

"Ode to the West Wind" is an ode, written by Percy Bysshe Shelley in 1819 in Cascine wood near Florence, Italy. It was originally published in 1820 by Charles Ollier in London as part of the collection *Prometheus Unbound, A Lyrical Drama in Four Acts, With Other Poems*. I'll need to order this book soon.

CHRISTMAS EVE

It's Christmas Eve
and I'm feeling nostalgic.
Yearning for days gone by.
When days were measured in
hours and minutes,
not statistics and polls.

When melancholy overpowers
cheerfulness and joy in my heart,
I look into the eyes of my grandkids.
There I find happiness.

Oh I wish I had known my grandfathers.
Grandpa Adolph died in 1922 in Chicago.
Grandpa Ivan passed in the 1960s
somewhere in California.
I yearn for a moment's glance from their eyes.
Pictures on the shelf will have to do.
I stare, but fail to pull their love into
my heart.

My quest, as yet another holiday
and year passes by, is to give my grandchildren
the gift of pleasant memories,
glancing deeply into their eyes
and occupying special spots
in their hearts.

Christmas Day 2022. The Blomberg family living in Wisconsin gathered at the homestead for a present opening under the tree harvested down by Vera's pond earlier in the month. Swedish glogg for son Karl and I. Two large tenderloins and all the fixings on the dinner table. Ten-year-old granddaughter Peyton is boycotting pork these days - she loves pigs - so the ham will be prepared on New Year's Eve when we all gather together again along the creek.

BIRTH OF AN OAK

*Imagine an acorn. Come
October falling to the ground.*

*Buried by a squirrel before
November's end.*

*Dormant underground from
December to April.*

Escaping hungry squirrels,

It sprouts in May.

*Spreads leafy wings from
June to August.*

January 1

A new year. My sixty-eighth New Year's Day. Born in 1954, I do not remember the early ones. Can't remember my first new year celebration. Perhaps after my eighteenth, when I could legally drink champagne? You see, back in 1972, eighteen was considered the legal age for drinking alcohol. We as a generation proved them wrong. Go figure. This year, I brought in the present year with my 10 year old granddaughter Peyton. Proof non-alcoholic sparkling grape champagne is safe for all ages.

"Love all, trust a few, do wrong to none." ~Shakespeare

January 5

The week's coming to an end with above normal temperatures. There has been snow on the ground since Thanksgiving. The days are getting longer. The long range temperature outlook is for above normal temperatures. Moisture in the clouds following the jet stream from the saturated west coast promises above normal precipitation here in the upper midwest. More snow? More ice? Time will tell. And hopefully, Vera's Pond should be full come March.

January 7

Two days left of the upland bird hunting season. The snow depth keeps me from the woods, so time for a drive-about this afternoon and tomorrow. Turkeys on the prowl for corn and acorns along the edge of woodlands, grouse working mature aspen and wayward stocked pheasants on public hunting grounds. Since the latter ones are too far away in southern parts of our state, it'll have to be searching for turkey and grouse on the fringes closer to home.

January 10

The sound of a chainsaw can be heard south of the kennel today. A logger has begun harvesting somewhere in the neighborhood of 5 acres of maturing aspen, maple, birch and basswood on our property. Felix is his name and he comes from Ridge Road, two miles to the southeast. Recommended by the County Forester, he and I have been working together for nearly 2 years to make this happen. Health problems slowed him down for a while, but trees are falling as we speak. With this opening in the woods, I anticipate a male woodcock or two returning in the spring to perform their courtship display. Hopefully, it may attract females to nest and raise broods in adjacent cover.

As discussed, logging around 5 acres of our woods is in progress. It's called a clear cut. Everything but a few oaks, white pine and hemlock will be removed and sent to the local mills. For my non-hunting friends, you may ask why? Regeneration of aspen and other young forest growth will sprout during the upcoming summer. Young aspen will spring forth from the root system of the harvested mature aspen. By the thousands. In a couple of years it will be near impossible to walk through the newly created and dense young forest. Come March and April, the newly created opening in the woods will attract a host of young forest wildlife, including our beloved woodcock.

We have always had woodcock sky dance and raise young here along the creek. We have banded many in the spring. But the past two seasons we did not record any breeding activity on our 40. Why? The woods had matured to the point that it became unattractive to woodcock and other young forest wildlife. I have not seen a ruffed grouse on our property for several years. Perhaps the clear cut and young aspen will attract a drumming male grouse this year or next. The last time our 40 acres was logged off was in 1985. 38 years ago! So it was time. Stay tuned and I'll report back on the progress of our newly created aspen clear cut.

A heavy snowfall of 5 inches arrived last night. This, after a week of light sleet and rain and icy driveways. A bucket of sand from the town garage helped around the driveways bordering the kennel and front porch. Snowblowing the new snow on our four driveways, including the one leading to the kennel and my office took longer than normal with a sheet of ice under the fresh snow.

January 20

Logger Felix also found the recent snow problematic when trying to locate fallen pulp logs now covered. He has hauled 10 cords of pulp to the paper mill so far. Another 5 cord load of 10 foot bolts (sawlogs) to a sawmill in Vesper owned by Hamels. Nearly 50 years ago I ushered at a wedding for the owner's brother Ed. Small world indeed.

January 21

Heavy, wet snow can wreak havoc in the woods. Branches sag, pine needles catch and hold tons of snow, rendering their strength useless. White pine branches snap with ease. Tree saplings and brush of all stripes bend over and touch the ground. The wooden bridge on the powerline trail crossing our creek is currently blocked with branches. Rather than cutting them down, I'll wait until the next thaw when most should spring forth and point skyward once again. I can take you into our woods and to this day, show you some trees that never straightened out after a major heavy snowfall during deer season twenty years ago.

January 22

Took our big John Deere tractor with the back blade out of the shed yesterday and plowed snow off the trails around the prairie field, along the hedgerow, around Vera and Golden Ponds and in the cheese factory white pine woods. Trails the grandchildren like to follow as they visit their favorite spots on the homestead - the prairie field, hedgerow, Vera and Golden Ponds and the cheese factory white pine woods.

January 25

The Barred owls on the back 40 are hooting up a storm these nights. Last evening I heard one hoot three times before coming in the house after kennel chores. There's an old saying about three hoots. As far as I know, nobody I know died last night. Great horned owls incubate their eggs in late winter, not sure about the Barred. My guess is that the latter are breeding now and will lay eggs before the snowpack melts away. Our pair of Ravens flew by this morning. Towards the northeast and the woods they nested in last spring. Crows won't be working on their nests for another month or two. Ravens probably do likewise.

January 27

As January comes to a close, winter aims to rear its ugly frigid head. We'll be entering February with below zero wind chills for daytime highs. Considering how mild January was this year, it seems we will be paying the price for last month's comfort. Hopefully the groundhog will give us good news next week and spring will indeed come early.

January 30

Was greeted out the kitchen window this morning by a group of five deer crossing our prairie field down by Vera's Pond. I ate a bagel with cream cheese, washed down by a second cup of coffee while they walked by single file. They came from the neighbor's corn field across the gravel road and headed into our woods where an active clearcut provided them fresh browse from residual tree tops. Despite the current sub-zero cold snap, our local deer are faring well. Dare I say, gaining weight?

January 31

Last day of January. My late father Adolph's birthday. He would have been 98 years old today. Property tax day. The day after granddaughter Peyton's birthday.

"The spoken word can never be taken back." ~Dad

"On Candlemas Day the bear, badger, or woodchuck comes out to see his shadow at noon: if he does not see it, he remains out; but if he does see it, he goes back to his hole for six more weeks, and cold weather continues for six weeks longer."
~Weather Lore - Richard Inwards

Groundhog Day. Candlemas Day. The bear, badger, woodchuck and groundhog all saw their shadows. As our local meteorologist said, on a normal year, in six weeks it'll be mid-March when our snow disappears and spring arrives. And I might add, that's when woodcock return from their southern wintering grounds.

February 4

A trip west to Eau Claire to visit friends Dan and Rita, Jim and Esta, and Ron and Connie. It's a location that forty years ago beaconed us during the pheasant and quail hunting seasons. Wild birds and bird dogs were a great combination back then and filled up a weekend or two. This weekend, we reminisced. And talked of dogs of yesteryears, getting old, and grandkids.

February 8

It's still winter along the creek. Snow blankets the landscape, with scattered patches of bare ground on fields where wind blew off a layer or two. Temperatures are moderating as the sun rises higher and daylight lingers longer each day. I can hose down kennel runs now that temperatures are above freezing. Sitting on a bar stool looking towards the sun, I felt the promise of spring on my face. The power of sun rays against the skin is remarkable indeed. A month from now, we'll be spending considerable time on the deck overlooking the prairie field as it warms up and awakens from its long, cold winter nap.

TIRED OF COLD

I'm tired of cold.
Perhaps it relates to my getting old.
The reason several million northern
elderly folk head south for the winter.
And why, except for ice fishers, skiers
and snowmobilers, sensible folks
remain indoors by the fire.
When I wore a younger man's clothes
I shed the cold much better.
Once snowshoed and camped deep
into Michigan's Porcupine Mountains.
Cross country skied on hills meant for goats.
Trapped for beaver, otter,
muskrats and mink below the ice.
Drilled holes for fish, snowmobiled
and hunted grouse and rabbits
until winter turned to spring.
Yes, I once embraced whatever
winter sent my way.
The older I got, the colder I got,
and became weary of getting cold.
But when the thermometer
reaches 32, all bets are off.
I load up the UTV with chainsaw,
grandma and the grandkids,
head for the pond, the creek
and the woods.
"It's too nice outside to be inside."
she'd say.
There's a trail needing brushing.
Sledding down a small hill by the pond.

Trees to climb and forts to build in the woods.
Memories to make. Traditions to maintain.
Standing on the edge of winter and
beckoning spring and warm weather to arrive.

February 11

44 degrees today. Sunny and spring-like warm. Sat on the kennel deck for a while before taking recyclables to the town garage. Took a "shortcut" home down Maple and River Roads. Once again the big river is wide open with only narrow ice shelves along the banks. Diving ducks like Goldeneyes and Mergansers are stacking up along this stretch of the river below the Dubay dam. Watching them dive and feed on minnows and fish is quite entertaining - to say the least.

February 15

Rain in February? Unseasonably warm weather - twenty degrees above average - causes peculiar weather patterns. Warmer westerly winds bring Pacific ocean moisture as opposed to colder northerly winds from the arctic circle. So it goes, rain in February. Disappearing snow cover on the backyard and back 40 signals spring is on the horizon. Reports are coming in of sandhill cranes crossing the southern border of our state and resting on last fall's harvested fields of corn.

Rain in February?

Look to the sky,

Winds from the south,

Clouds full of water,

Sure to melt the snow,

Warmer temps on tap,

Two weeks to March,

Look to the sky,

Rain in February?

No balloons in sight.

February 16

Spring seems to be the best time to expect a litter of puppies. New life and bringing another member into the family. Twice a year our female dogs come into season and this year is no exception. Mitzie, the 3-year old daughter of our beloved Buster, is prime for breeding this week. Raven, our new male cocker spaniel will be the father of this potential spring litter. Fingers crossed that all goes well.

February 17

As fate would have it, our cockers mated today. If all goes as planned, puppies should arrive 2 months from now in mid-April. Nothing like spring puppies, happy grandchildren and elated new owners. Just shy of fifty years breeding gun dogs has taught me well the joys that come with litters of puppies.

"Whoever said you can't buy happiness never bought a puppy."
~Gene Hill

Snow should return to our state in a big way this week. The first wave hit this afternoon with a few inches, more tomorrow and by Friday, possibly up to 20 inches. That would be the largest snowfall of this winter season. Time will tell. Woke up this morning to the sounds of happy birthday, as the boss celebrates her 66th trip around the sun. The whole family is here for the duration of the upcoming snowstorm, so out for breakfast at grandmother's favorite breakfast restaurant. And dinner this evening prepared by No. 2 son Karl.

Olivia arrived here on Tuesday. It's Thursday and she packed a second punch today. You see, she's a winter storm and when they produce heavy snow, high winds and blizzard conditions, weather folks seem to give them names - Olivia is this one's moniker. She left us somewhere in the neighborhood of 14 inches with drifts up to 2 feet. It was a two-time snowblower event. And we suddenly found ourselves back into winter mode.

Our logger pulled out yesterday before the snow got too deep. And boy, did the deer pull in. Day and night they browse on treetop residue left on the forest floor. Before and after the storm. The trail camera verifies the fact that deer increase their food consumption during periods of inclement weather events. Very little activity at a second camera positioned by Golden Pond. Many bucks still sport their antlers.

In his book *The Old Man and the Sea*, Hemingway wrote, "The old man left the smell of the land behind and sailed out into the clean early morning smell of the ocean." To that I say, the smell of the land varies by location. Prairie fields smell different than piney woods, which smell different than aspen woods, or an oak covered ridge-line, or alder bottoms, or an October corn-field. So much so, that one can close their eyes and know where they are outdoors by simply smelling.

February 28

Leap years, every 4 years have an extra day - February 29 - but not this year.

MARCH

Who among us does not rejoice with the onset of spring?
Melting snow, honking geese, dabbling ducks, the first blackbird or robin
and the sweet, fresh aroma only spring air can provide.
These are but a few of the early signs we've seen during the change of seasons.

For those of us that live in the land of four true seasons,spring has a deeper, personal meaning.It's a time to celebrate the homecoming of creatures that inhabit our woods and fields for no more than six, or seven months. That includes a host of migrant birds – their numbers too numerous to list in this space. Local resident creatures that survived winter's wrath emerge from the recesses of deep woods and swamps – either from hibernation or solitude - and live to reproduce once again.

Suddenly in March, the sun stays up at the end of the day until well past seven. The extra hour of sunshine granted for energy's sake by the rascals on the east coast means little to our cardinals - whose biological clocks operate by foot-candles of sunlight,not daylight savings. The sun rises and sets at the same time each day as far as they are concerned. Despite weekly schedules and alarm clock settings, sunrise and sunset are still measured at our home by the exact time the cardinals start and end their days at the feeders.

March 1

Experts concur that a pleasant physical chemical reaction occurs when we are exposed to more daylight and warmer temperatures in spring. I delight in the notion that wild creatures also feel better this time of year. As demeanors improve and spirits rise, so too does one's energy level. I suppose that is reason enough to allow us some extra, end of the day outdoor time. Perhaps this time, something worthwhile has trickled out of Washington, D.C.

March 2

I've watched the snow melt and the rain fall for fifty springs along this stretch of the Wisconsin River valley. Each and every year, with few exceptions, spring reveals much more than it leaves behind. In recent years, young sturgeons now congregate to spawn below the dam at Dubay. Black bears, rolling out of their deep winter slumber, were once considered a rare sight in our neighborhood – but are now thought to be common. Canada geese formerly flew by in the spring on their way to northern breeding grounds. These days, they stop and raise families on local ponds and backwater sloughs. Gulls have colonized islands on nearby flowages and fly over the house on a regular basis. Flocks of turkeys, in numbers surpassing the abundant deer herd, were non-existent here in the past – as were fishers, who made their presence known a few springs ago in our chicken coop. Eagles used to be seen on occasion, but are now almost daily visitors flying over our property. And turkey vultures often circle the neighborhood, searching for roadkill. Oh, and did I mention wolves that visit on occasion?

When the snow melts and the ground thaws out some time later this month, woodcock will return after their long journey from southern wintering grounds. Perhaps from as far as Louisiana. Should one or more decide to stop here, then our property becomes part of their northern breeding grounds. Much to our delight and to that of our bird dogs, woodcock live and dine here for nearly seven months of the year. Spring is currently taking its good natured time this year. Several early March snowfalls have covered up any signs of seasonal change. A pair of Canada geese flew over the kennel this weekend and landed across the gravel road on the neighbor's backwater slough.

March 5

An owl, an eagle and a pair of geese. Our male nuthatches and cardinals have changed from winter to springtime tunes. Today, I was greeted with a melody from returning geese - then an owl plunging from a white pine onto a snowbound rodent - and finally, a bald eagle fending off a pair of crows along our east property line. The crows won, driving the eagle away from their nest in the oaks. I wonder where the eagle's nest is located?

March 14

The past two spring snowstorms left us a total of nearly 12 inches on the ground - that on top of some older snow. Yesterday's new layer brought snowbanks along the house and kennel driveways to new heights. Snow depths this winter and spring are well above normal, leaving smiles on area snowmobilers and skiers. A lone robin and a lone blackbird are hanging out at our backyard bird feeders - and like us, hoping for warmer temperatures and melting snow.

March 15

Spring woodcock migration from southern states is fueled by daylight, wind and the urge to mate. Male birds actively perform their courtship "sky dance" in likely spots along their way north. Spring and fall, they feed and loaf in sheltered coverts during the day and migrate after dark. Traveling at heights of somewhere between 50 to several hundred feet, depending on wind direction and speed, they can cover 30 to 500 miles a day, alone, or in loose flocks - often called "flights." All along the route, male woodcock set up shop at openings in the woods - called singing grounds - next to suitable nesting habitats that attract females.

"Don't let anyone tell you that getting old happens in the autumn of your life. It happens in March."
~Robert Ruark - The Old Man and the Boy

March 16

Hopefully, a male woodcock or two, most likely following the river valley, will arrive and claim one of several singing grounds on our property. Our new 5-acre clearcut should attract both male and female woodcock. Males have begun dancing in the sky at dusk each evening, hoping to lure any early arriving females.

Some early spring males are migrants on their way to more northerly breeding grounds. They pick up favorable winds and continue up the Wisconsin River valley until they hit the south shore of Lake Superior, where they most likely follow a northwesterly direction to somewhere in Minnesota, or Canada.

March 17

Two years after clear-cutting mature aspen stands, around 5,000 aspen root suckers should appear per acre. Some cuts may have up to 70,000 root suckers per acre. The more root suckers, the better, because aspen stands naturally thin themselves out.

March 18

Five senses. Smell, sight, touch, hearing and taste. Each of mine carries a different meaning according to the season. Air smells different in spring. Different in summer, fall and winter. Air carries the scent of all things seasonable. Like the aroma of lilac flowers in spring, freshly cut grass in summer, burning leaves in fall and woodsmoke in winter. Watching skeins of spring geese, trout rising for a hatch of flies in June, a fall of woodcock in October and snow piling deep in mid-winter. The feel of radiant sun as winter turns to spring, forehead sweat of summer and the bite of autumn frost on one's fingertips. Who among us does not marvel at the sound of spring drumming grouse, summer whippoorwills echoing from the distant edge of a woodlot, the raspy calls from migrating nighthawks in fall and owls hooting from snow covered pines. And the taste of fresh cut asparagus in spring, summer's sweet corn, pumpkin pie in fall and hot cocoa on days remain below zero in winter.

March 20

Spring officially begins today. The entire world experiences the same amount of daylight and darkness on this date. So there you have it, despite the fact that there's a half a foot of snow on the ground and spring migrant birds are holding off farther south where bare ground is available. We're feeding mealworms to a couple of robins on the driveway to carry them through until spring's real arrival.

WOODCOCK SONG

When it comes to secrets,
no other upland game bird
comes close to mystery as
the upland prince woodcock.

From dusk to dawn they fly
under cover of darkness.
From dawn to dusk they
rest and feed in clumps of
aspen, alder, willow and
dogwood.

North in spring, south in fall.
With strong tailwinds and
updrafts able to climb over 7800
feet and travel more than 600
miles in a single night.

From northern states and
southern provinces they
migrate each fall, to eastern
seaboard states, Gulf
shores and eastern Texas.

Spring urges them back to
northern breeding grounds.
To sing and dance at
places of beginning;
a mysterious ritual indeed.

*There, males dance to
attract a mate or two.
High in the sky they circle,
then fall back to earth to
twitter and peent their
love struck song.*

*A ritual repeated every
spring, witnessed by a
fortunate few. Nature's
way of replenishing
alder bottoms each fall;
delighting hunters and
bird dogs alike.*

My wife's father passed away this weekend. Even at 96, it was still a surprise, as he was feeling normal a day earlier. He had a serious stroke and ended up in the hospital's intensive care unit where the family gathered at his bedside for final goodbyes. I could write a book about John, as his life was a colorful, ongoing story. Working in the state corrections system, hunting, fishing and trapping in the outdoors, growing up during the Great Depression, serving our country during WWII and raising a large family. The following is a poem I wrote the day he passed away.

A SHOOTING STAR

A trio of mallards flew by,
cutting through a historic snowstorm,
and landed in the river. A lone male merganser
was looking for a lost mate. All three swam under the
river bridge beside the downtown hospital. From a second
story intensive care window, I watched ducks and gulls battling
the storm as my 96 year old father-in-law lay nearby, battling death.

How fitting. There lie a WWII veteran,
prison warden and retired Chief of Security of
our state prison system. An honest to goodness warrior.
As a Depression child, born and raised in Wautoma, he hunted,
trapped and fished to make good money and help feed his family. He loved
the woods and lumber. Like his father, he was a masterful woodworker.
His talents
ran deep. The cabinets, ceilings, door frames and walls of our house all
bear his signature.

I married one of his daughters.
He and his wife had six children -
three boys and three girls. As parents they
were strict. As spouses devoted. As grandparents
adored. Their will reads, "Bury us on a Saturday, so nobody
has to take off from work." Right up to the end, he was sharp as
a tack. Wautoma lost a historian. He recalled the people, places and
history of his hometown like no other. He will surely be missed by family
and friends. Missed indeed, but never forgotten.

On the way home from the
hospital that night, driving west on
Highway 10, my wife and I both saw a
shooting star falling from the sky. It's thought
that shooting stars are signs that someone who's left the
physical world is still with you - and that person is encouraging
you to continue living your life being the best you that you can. I saw a
shooting star the night my own father passed away, thirty-some years ago.
I always thought that was a message from him. Now, I know it's worth
believing.

March 28

A pair of Sandhill cranes appeared on our Clearcut trail camera today. They either flew in by way of the new landing strip created by removing several acres of our woods, or they walked in on the trail that leads to that point by way of the Original Pond. No matter how they arrived, they will be added to the list of creatures utilizing our habitat management project.

March 29

A large male bobcat passed by our Golden Pond trail camera

at 1:15 am this morning. We got word from our neighbors west and east of our home that a pair had been seen on their property. Our picture stands as proof one visited our land and joins the family's long life list of documented visiting and resident critters.

March 31

The month is coming to an end and is still rumbling like a lion. Snow storms, freezing rain, thunderstorms and occasional upper 40 degree temperatures.

April 1

No fooling. It's April, and at times it feels like December. Snow still fills the woods. Temperatures struggle to rise above freezing. Snow, sleet, freezing rain and high winds in the forecast. Long range weather predictions have been more of the same. 40 degree days are welcome. The 50s are a dream. The old standbys have arrived. Geese, redwing blackbirds, robins, cranes and divers on the river.

April 3

Woodcock return. There have been reports south of here, but a back 40 male sang on our training field this evening. Karl and Peyton heard his peenting. For me, that's the official beginning of spring along the creek.

April 5

With an anticipated litter of cocker puppies due on the 22nd of this month, I needed to find a vet able to remove dew claws and dock tails on the pups at 72 hours after birth. My long standing local vet of choice for this duty passed away last year, so finding one close to home was in order. Near my inlaws in Wautoma was one that was recommended by another breeder. So a visit was in order today during a visit with Lynda's mother. Turns out this vet has two offices - with one in Bancroft, much closer to home. We hope to get on their calendar with the expected dates presumed later this month.

April 9

Easter Sunday. We ate our ham, sweet potatoes, baked beans and broccoli casserole yesterday since we were alone and hungry for Easter fixings all weekend long. The grandkids were sick at their home in Coloma. My wife was preparing for the arrival of son Erik and grandson Carson from Maine later this week. A reunion of cousins and a woodcock banding event is planned.

April 10

Listened for singing woodcock last night on the new clear-cut. Nothing heard except several owls, geese, cranes and a few spring frogs. Ice is almost gone from the ponds. This week's fore-casted record high temperatures of around 80 degrees will make the ice a memory and will awaken a chorus of frogs numbering hundreds by week's end. Did you know, all toads are frogs, but not all frogs are toads?

April 11

Karl and I listened for woodcock at dusk tonight. He and grandson Wyatt heard one yesterday evening to the east of the house. We not only heard one, but saw 2 flying over our prairie field and displaying near the hedgerow. I could not hear them peenting, as the noise from spring peepers and wood frogs was deafening and made my weak hearing worthless.

April 12

The river came to flood stage last night and this morning.

River Road remains dry, but the water has risen to the top of the river banks.

April 13

No. 1 son and No. 2 grandson flew into central Wisconsin tonight from east central Maine. A combined family visit along with a woodcock banding project brought them both here for a week's visit. Son Erik is a Professor of Wildlife at the University of Maine in Orono. He spearheaded the Eastern Woodcock Migration Research Cooperative along with twenty-eight agency partners from several Canadian Provinces to southern states like Georgia and Florida. You see, American Woodcock migrate every spring and fall to breed and winter in warmer climates. And Erik, along with a host of his graduate students, state agency personnel and volunteers, have placed satellite transmitters on the birds to track their movements. And he came here to place two transmitters on birds his father, friend Mike and UW-Stevens Point Wildlife Society students plan to capture over the next few days.

SPRING

I know it has happened before,
but for this aging heart
it bears repeating.

Springs come and go
here in the north
with little fanfare.
Snow melts,
Rivers flow strong,
Robins return,
Grass greens up,
Geese and cranes trumpet
and we all wait patiently for bluebirds,

orioles and hummingbirds. As I walked out the back porch towards the
kennels on the tenth of April, three male turkeys, still on roost, gobbled
for the first time to prospective mates. Then on the thirteenth, again on
the porch,
wearing three layers of spring outerwear,
I was struck by what seemed like
late October weather.
When the leaves had fallen and
northwest winds bring a chilling frost.
Snowflakes in the forecast,
Geese and cranes trumpeting,
Robins migrating,
Bluebirds, orioles and hummingbirds have disappeared.
It snowed on the fourteenth.
but it is spring by way of the calendar.
On the fifteenth a bluebird arrived.
Then, on the sixteenth,
I was met by a lone scout swallow
cruising the prairie field out back.
Looking for flying insects,
watching for straggling relatives,
hoping for a hatch. So goes spring along the creek once again.......

April 17

This evening our Wisconsin Woodcock Research Project team captured woodcock WI2023001 and was fitted with a satellite transmitter, measured, weighed and banded. It was released into the darkness and began sending valuable information to woodcockmigration.org researchers. It was a female bird, so we expect her to nest here in central WI and remain close to her nest and chicks. The satellite transmitter will tell us the story of her spring and summer activities and fall migration route south.

April 19

American Woodcock WI2023002, a male, was caught, equipped with a satellite transmitter and released tonight. That on the heels of WI2023001's release a few days ago. The birds' equipment will "wake up" in a few days and then tracking their movements will begin.

April 21

Updates. Female WI2023001 has sent a transmission. On 4/16 and 4/18 she was still on our 40 acre banding site near Bancroft, WI and about 100 yards from the landowner's workshop. On 4/20 she was 250 miles northwest in Minnesota by Mille Lacs, and at midnight tonight (4/21) she moved 40 miles east to Sturgeon Lake, Minnesota. It's apparent we caught a female that was still migrating north. Stay tuned as we discover her final nesting site, wherever that might be.

Male WI2023002 is still in our study area near Bancroft, WI - approximately 300 feet from the point of capture. He moved a few hundred feet northwest and has been hanging out near his singing grounds. Unlike the female WI2023001, who left soon after capture to Minnesota, he remains here in Wisconsin.

April 22

Puppies arrived today! Ours, a fine litter of field bred English Cocker Spaniels were presented to us this morning by our sweet female Mitzie, daughter of our beloved Buster. The sire is our new, up and coming male Raven. Puppies are all alive and doing well. Granddaughter Peyton has her eyes on one of these puppies. Stay tuned.

Trip south to the veterinarian. Esta and Jim Olson greeted Karl, Peyton and I carrying a postal box full of 3-day old cocker spaniel puppies. The mission was a health check and to dock their tails and remove dew claws from their front legs. Forty-some years of breeding and care of German Shorthaired Pointers and English Cockers included this necessary procedure. Not only does it comply with existing breed standards, but assures the dogs safety from injuries afield as adults.

April 25

Arrived at Jimmy's and Esta's horse ranch on the Kickapoo River in Monroe County this evening for the start of turkey camp 2023. This marks nearly four decades of hunting this Driftless Area with good friends Jim and Dan. Years ago, we introduced my sons to the challenges of pursuing wild turkeys in this hill country of southwestern Wisconsin. A tradition so strong, our host Jim built a small cabin at his place to accommodate good friends for as long as they care to stay. And here we are today, once again.

April 26

Just moments before 4 am, the alarm and the sound of Jim entering the cabin with a fresh pot of hot coffee was enough to start the day. Arriving at the blinds Jim built on top of his 60 acre property before dawn has been our routine for many years. The blinds are positioned on the ridge crossing the top of his land and is accessible by truck on an off-road, two track trail. There he dropped us off near our stands - one for Dan and one for me. After hiding the truck he joined Dan in the lower blind. I was nestled in my blind, sipping on a second cup of coffee when I heard the first gobbling. Three toms were still roosting in tall white pines over "Carrie's Point" to the east. As the sun rose, their mating calls became more frequent - until they flew down to the ground on the hilltop field we occupied. Sounding like they were moving further east, they eventually went silent. I relaxed and poured another cup of coffee from my thermos.

Then it happened. Out of the corner of my eye I caught motion. In single file, the three male gobblers marched past my blind at 25 yards. I raised my shotgun and aimed at the largest lead bird. No time to get nervous, I pulled the trigger. And missed! He took flight, unharmed and flew over Jim's and Dan's blind. It's been a long time since I've missed a twenty-five pound turkey - and such an easy shot taboot! Later, after the obligatory ribbing, Jim suggested I get a scope for my shotgun. "Take away the guesswork," he remarked. "Just put the crosshairs on his head."

April 30

Woodcock update - The female WI2023001 is still in MN, but has moved another 15 miles NE and is near Mahtowa, not too far from Cloquet. She had locations on the 24th, 26th, 28th, 30th within 100 yards of each other, so maybe she is settling in. It looks like a nice piece of young forest, maybe even being managed by the landowner.

The male WI2023002 was still on Mike's property (where it was captured) as of 4-29. Very close to the same cluster of locations transmitted earlier. We got new signals from him on the 23rd, 25th, and 29th, but missed a location on the 27th. It's possible we might recover that one with future downloads. The bird seems to be holding tight to an area of about 20-30 yards or so - which is well within the range of normal.

My son Erik's and his grad student Rachel just got back from West Virginia, where they put out 17 transmitters in 5 nights! She'll get back to their regular schedule of doing weekly downloads of the entire dataset this week. Since they seem to be functioning well, he'll send more updates on them when he gets Rachel's weekly updates on the whole dataset.

"To band a bird is to hold a ticket in a great lottery."
~Aldo Leopold - A Sand County Almanac - 65290

May 6

I turned 69 years old today. One year away from 70. My father lived for 71 years. His father, my grandfather, only lived to be 48. My other grandfather, my mother's father, lived for 65 years. That said, my mother lived to be 97. So, take that for what it's worth. I think I'm good for 85 years.

May 7

Tree planting. A family affair. Today with Karl, Meghan and three grandkids - Peyton, Wyatt and Rykar. Nina and Papa bought firs, tamaracks, maples, crabapples, and ashes. Planted some future christmas trees alongside a stand of red pines planted thirty years ago with young sons Erik and Karl. The Mountain Ashes and Crabapples were planted in a semicircle near a fire pit and Leopold benches alongside Vera's Pond. Others were planted near graves of dogs Buster and Belle. A few others across the road by Karl's and Meghan's potential future home site. Still remaining to plant near Golden Pond are some tamarack.

May 10

The leaves of the roselow crabapple, silky dogwood and ninebark are turning green, making the 626 foot hedgerow that splits the eastern half of our prairie field stand out against the dead brown grass remaining after the long winter months. The cost share investment we made with the county's Central Wisconsin Windshare Partners is coming to fruition.

The Cocker puppies turned three weeks old today. The boss helped me with the worming process this morning. Next week we'll introduce solid food as we prepare to start weaning them from mother Mitzie. They're all looking good and developing right on schedule.

The last of this year's tree planting was accomplished today. Ten tamaracks were set on the east side of the trail passing by the Original Pond. These slow growing deciduous pines will mature when I'm about 129 years old. Or, when my sons are in their 80s, my grandchildren in their 50s, my great grandchildren in their 30s, and my great-great grandchildren in their teens. Tamaracks are truly generational trees. And come each future fall, they will turn Leopold's smokey gold before losing their needles.

Today I traveled to the east side of the Wisconsin River to Gollon's fish farm. There I purchased 50 hybrid bluegill and 50 perch for planting in Vera's Pond. In addition, I bought a gallon of minnows and fish pellets to ensure the introduced fish would eat well. When the timing is right, we'll transplant many of them into Golden Pond.

Well, the first fishing excursion at Vera's Pond was a bust. The grandchildren failed to get even one nibble using worms and bobbers. Apparently the small panfish sought refuge in last year's remaining cattails. The instinct to hide from predators overcame any hunger pains they may have at this time. In time, I suggest, and as they grow, they will begin biting on our grandkids' offerings.

The first day of my second turkey hunting season began today. A three hour sit this morning in a blind along the creek revealed only three deer and a gray squirrel. No gobbles or clucks were heard. But a brief nap sure felt good on this brisk 40 degree morning.

May 19

Our oldest son turned 40 today. Oh my! A minor shock to wake up and realize you have a child turning 40. More of an eye opener than when I turned 69 earlier this month. And tomorrow our "youngest" son turns 35. Time slips by before our very eyes. And in 16 years when I turn 85, our oldest granddaughter will be 26. Oh my!

SIMPLE PLEASURES

Skipping stones.
Collecting pine cones.
Gathering feathers.
Catching tadpoles.
Picking mushrooms.
Cutting asparagus.
Counting butterflies.
Dodging dragonflies.
Watching swallows.
Blowing bubbles.
Picking dandelions.
Circling campfires.
Eating S'mores.
Roasting marshmallows. Just a few grandparent pastimes.

We buried good family friend and mentor Glen Rutz today. Like a second father, I knew him and his late wife Gloriette since grade school. Their oldest son is the brother I never had. We grew up together and still remain close after all these years. Glen was 95 and lived a long and outstanding life. An outdoorsman until the end, he showed Mike, his two brothers and me the ropes. Taught us how to handle guns and bows safely and appreciate all that Mother Nature had to offer. He reminded us that "There are two types of people in this world, givers and takers. You should strive to be a giver." Rest in peace Glen, and give Gloriette a hug for me.

May 21

Smokey skies overhead are a result of wildfires in western Canada. A high pressure "omega block" sets over Alberta, Saskatchewan and British Columbia and is setting record high temperatures. The area produces large quantities of crude oil and they now predict an increase in gas prices across North America.

May 22

This morning, as I headed to morning chores at the kennel, a large flock of Canada geese - numbering perhaps 35 - flew off the neighbor's picked corn field. They headed southeast and towards the River, exercising their wings and voices and raising all sorts of clamor. The local goose numbers continue to grow, adding to what biologists call Wisconsin's Mississippi Valley Population (MVP) flock. It's the reason we now have an early goose hunting season beginning September 1st.

May 26

The kennel is filling up with visitors on this Memorial Day weekend. Four dogs today, and two yesterday. Ours is a small boarding kennel, with a normal capacity of up to six dogs. If need be, an overflow of a couple more dogs can be handled. To that end, son Karl is updating six inside kennels that were usually reserved for my personal dogs. Two of those, Raven and Mitzie now live in our house. Seven puppies currently fill the attached whelping room. They will leave us in 3 weeks. This may be our last litter after nearly 50 years of raising German Shorthaired Pointers and English Cocker Spaniels. It's a bittersweet transition from raising and training gun dogs to strickly boarding, yet heartwarming knowing our children and grandchildren may take over the kennel business in the years to come.

A Day in the Life of an Old Retired Guy

6am- wake up, coffee, morning news.

7am- take a drive down River Rd, release a nuisance raccoon from a live trap - spot three turkeys on a neighbor's field.

8am- shower, dress, out to the kennel to do morning chores, feed dogs.

9am- drive UTV down to turkey blind.

10am- call in 3 jakes and a hen to within 50 yards of blind. Watch the 4 for one hour until they head back across the road.

11 am- back to the kennel office, work on book 2 manuscript.

Noon - welcome and check-in 2 boarders, Moose and Gus, and the owners.

1 pm- handle repeat breeding of English cockers

2pm- conference call with the banker and the "boss".

3pm- The dog and I take a nap.

4pm- afternoon kennel chores, feed dogs. Cut grass in the front yard.

5pm- drive to the neighborhood bar for fish fry and old fashioned happy hour.
6pm- back home. Watch the news.
7pm- to be determined. There's a woodcock singing out back, begging to be banded, turkeys gobbling in the neighbor's woods, begging to be located, more grass to cut, a recliner calling my name.
10pm- evening kennel chores, exercise and put dogs to bed.
11 pm- recliner and a night cap....

May 29

Seventeen geese flew over the house this morning while I was finishing my second cup of coffee. Last year's young birds, waiting to mature, are now hanging out together, waiting out the summer. Adult pairs are tending to this year's goslings on borrow ponds along the new four-lane highway and beaver ponds in the woods.

June 1

The puppies have now turned 5 weeks, going on 6, and their mother has left the whelping box for good. The transition from mother's milk to soft puppy chow went well and they're eating 3 times a day. They now average about 4-5 pounds. A second worming has been accomplished and by the time they reach the new owners' hands, they will have been treated 3 times. Their first puppy shot will also be given early in the week they leave. They will be leaving for their future homes around Saturday, June 17th - the day they turn 8 weeks old.

June 3

And then the weather turned dry. Fires rage in Canada. From Alberts to Ontario, sending smoke across the border resulting in eerie haze and air pollution across the northern states - including Wisconsin. The normal green treeline at the end of the prairie field turned smoky gray for the better part of last week. Jet stream winds have shifted, sending the smoke plumes towards the east coast.

June 7

Last night we had an unwelcome visitor. A black bear bent and tipped over two of the boss's bird feeders. For weeks, she religiously took in the suet and jelly feeders at night. She even set an alarm for around 9 pm to remind her to do so. Then she admitted to getting lazy. "Oh well," she lamented. "It was my fault I guess."

June 6

"I'm seriously thinking about buying a gun," she said while sitting at the kitchen table looking over her east side bird feeders. That's all it took for me to grab my coffee cup and a couple of shells for the 20 gauge single shotgun in the corner of the front entryway. I took a stand on the front porch and waited. It only took 10 minutes for the first red squirrel to appear below one of the feeders. He or she never knew what hit him or her. I was left to wonder, "Maybe I should let her buy a gun before I shoot any more?"

June 8

The lack of rain locally has caused Vera's pond to drop 2 inches. Time to pump from the old cheese factory well through the drain pipe into the pond. And with luck, enough rainfall from the kennel roof gutters, drain pipe and below surface groundwater will help to replenish the pond.

"What was big was not the trout, but the chance. What was full was not my creel, but my memory."
~Aldo Leopold - The Alder Fork - A Fishing Idyl

June 30

After a lifetime listening to their melodies, I only recently realized I couldn't match all bird voices to their names. Like the red bellied woodpecker who greeted me this morning by our front deck. Climbing the woodpecker pole he sounded a trademark drumming call. Aldo Leopold woke up often before daylight in the early morning to record what he referred to as a dawn chorus. In order he'd hear robins, doves, cardinals, flycatchers, catbirds and wrens. So many birds, so many melodies.

July 1

There came a time in my life when I realized my sons knew more than I did. After too many "I know dad", I learned to choose my words of wisdom carefully going forward. Then came grandkids. "Eureka!" I thought. A new generation to share my stories, thoughts and wisdom. Before they grow old enough to realize they know more than the old man.

July 4

The fourth of July. Independence Day. A day of celebration. Time to gather by the river with friends, family and neighbors. Eat, drink and watch the evening fireworks. We did it every year until us old folks stopped liking the crowds, traffic jams and noise. So staying at home with the dogs was in order. And everything was alright until the neighbors down the road brought home suitcases loaded with fireworks.

Now we have an extended holiday with lots of noise after dark for several days before and after the 4th.

That would be ok, if we didn't have a kennel full of dogs - many of which are afraid of fireworks. Sigh…

July 10

It happened today. A perfect summer day. On a visit to the boss's mother's home in Wautoma. Partly cloudy, light breeze, back porch, cup of coffee, sliced cucumbers fresh from the garden. Under the retractable awning, I watched the songbirds at her feeders, the grandkids running barefoot across the well groomed lawn and billowing clouds against the dark blue sky. Norman Rockwell came to mind.

July 14

Sitting on the back porch with the boss yesterday I gazed skyward and watched small, scattered stratus clouds racing to the southeast. Following another wave of severe thunderstorms the night before, our rain gauge told the story. We had been spared more rain, wind damage and power outages that occurred north and south of our place along the creek. The speeding clouds caused a song to ring in my head. It was Bob Dylan's 1962 classic, Blowin' in the Wind. "How many times must a man look up before he can see the sky? The answer, my friend, is blowin' in the wind." I dare you to look at the lyrics of this nearly 60 year old song. Then reach with me for answers about freedom and death.

The great conservationist and hunter Aldo Leopold listened to geese and wind "blowing taps for summer" in his book, A Sand County Almanac. He watched geese disappear on southerly winds and dreamed he could too, "If I were the wind". Do yourself a favor and read, or re-read his Almanac. His land ethic includes words of wisdom on human ethics. Both in short supply these days.

Henry David Thoreau speculated that when things were at loose ends, "Who knows which way the wind will blow tomorrow?" John Muir once said, "The winds will blow their own freshness into you, and the storms their energy, while cares will drop away from you like the leaves of Autumn."

Thoreau, reminds us, "The morning wind forever blows, the poem of creation is uninterrupted; but few are the ears to hear it."

So, during these troubled times I urge you to stop what you're doing, and from time to time turn your face into the wind, close your eyes and listen. Your answers my friends, might just be blowin' in the wind.

July 15

The neighbors decided to celebrate the 4th again last night. I'm not sure how expensive fireworks are, but a month's mortgage payment and grocery bill went up in glory and smoke over the course of nearly an hour. I retreated to my kennel office to calm a couple of noise sensitive boarders with company and loud music.

July 17

"Buddy," the last cocker puppy from this year's litter was sold today. He went to a family that were already fans of field bred cocker spaniels. In fact, a young couple with two young children that have begun the journey of establishing a kennel in west central Wisconsin.

IF I WERE A BIRD DOG

If I were a bird dog
I'd never grow tired
searching for scent cones
floating in the wind
carrying sweet aroma
of autumn game birds
around every corner
out of sight in cover
reserved for hunters
and their bird dogs.

If I were a bird dog
I could hunt all day
hoping my master
would keep up and
aim true at flushed birds
so I could retrieve
mouthfuls of feathers
filling game bags with
meat for the table.
If I were a bird dog.

July 21

This is definitely the year of the Wild Bergamot. Across our prairie grass field this plant can be seen everywhere this year. Its pale lavender flowers stand out among the more plentiful yellow and white wild flowers. During a "nature ride" on grandma's new off road electric golf cart, while the grandkids scanned milkweeds for monarch caterpillars, No. 1 granddaughter spotted a hummingbird moth. A rare sighting indeed. I don't recall the last time I saw one. It was working over a Bergamot plant's flower cluster and buzzing from one clump to another with the speed of a feathered hummingbird. What a treat and today's highlight for sure.

July 22

Speaking of insects, did you know there are several hundred thousand varieties? Or that there may be more kinds of insects on one acre of land than species of birds in the entire United States? Perhaps as high as several million per acre! While many consider insects pests, many are quite beneficial and all serve a purpose in nature's pyramid.. Their pollination services alone are worth nearly $4.5 billion annually in our country. And as food sources for our feathered friends, they are indispensable.

July 23

The boss worries when I'm in the woods alone. Today I was on my tractor spreading gravel on the trail that borders our new aspen clearcut. Off to my left I noticed a young whitetail buck watching my every move. He barely moved as I brought and dumped load after load of gravel. I stopped long enough to snap a few pictures as he stared my way. "Not to worry dear," I thought. "I'm never alone in the woods."

"And into the forest I go, to lose my mind and find my soul."
~John Muir

August 1

Crickets are now serenading us on these warm humid nights. As summer disappears, so too will warm nights and the soothing chirp, chirp, chirp of courting nocturnal males. Singing away late summer and early fall nights – to nearby females and rival suitors. Habitually joined in harmony by a chorus of dozens, this year alas, only two – one out front, the other in our backyard. Perhaps the rest were victims of past drought years? Lore has it that crickets are a sign of things to come, good or bad - luck, rain, financial windfall, death, pregnancy, illness, or hope. It is said a love sick cricket may sing for hours at a time, as some people will regrettably attest. One very patient zoologist once documented a single cricket chirping no less than 42,000 times over a period of four hours. I, for one, relate their soothing song to impending autumn – my favorite time of the year. I just wish their ranks were stronger and the chorus louder!

SIT A SPELL

On this bench,
Along this river,
Enjoy the sights,
Relish the sounds.

Sit a spell,
Take a load off,
Catch your breath,
Watch the river slide by,
Spy an eagle gliding overhead,
Note fish rising to the surface.

Listen for geese,
and passing ducks,
Chatter from kingfishers,
tree-tapping woodpeckers,
screaming ospreys,
and raucous gulls.

Close your eyes,
Take a leisurely nap,
Hear the sounds of silence broken,
on occasion by river dwellers.
Beaver water slapping their flat tails,
otters slip sliding up and down banks,
muskrats foraging in backwater,
and mink hunting along river's edge.

Dream of times gone by,
and future things to come.
Return here any time you feel
the need to cleanse your mind
and soul. The river is happy to
share.

August 5

I told No.1 granddaughter crickets can tell us what the current temperature is - by listening and counting their chirps. According to experts, a rough estimate of the temperature in degrees Fahrenheit can be determined by counting the number of chirps in 15 seconds and then adding 37. The resulting number will be an approximation of the outside temperature. Imagine that!

August 7

Sad day along the creek. The family had to bury Finn, a 9th generation Eau Pleine German Shorthaired pointer. Son of Rocky and Sage, he represented 49 years of raising, training and caring for our own bloodline of this wonderful gun dog breed. By my recent count, he was one of 33 that resided in our kennel and home over these many years. More than thirty graves along the creek and back 40. Lots of memories and tears. Eight generations. Finn was buried this day among the rest.

August 8

Several logs from last winter's clearcut went to friend Mike's sawmill on the Buena Vista marsh. Karl loaded two large basswood and one maple on our trailer and I traveled south 30 miles to have them transformed into beams and lumber. Basswood beams will be made into smaller blocks, dried and carved into working duck decoys. Another retirement project underway.

August 12

A fly flew by the Woodpecker Inn today on the corner of Mayflower Road and County E. An Inn named no doubt after numerous wood pecking birds inhabiting the nearby forest. An Inn famous for cold beer, cheese curds and ice cream. Years ago, neighbor Cliff recalled as a young boy he'd stop for a scoop on his way home from a one-room schoolhouse on Maple Road. The Mayflower Cheese Factory, built in 1928 barely survived the Depression by attracting local dairy farmers, their children and passerby's - hungry for a curd, thirsty for a brew, or craving a cone. That, in fact, is why the cheesemaker built the adjoining Woodpecker Inn. Soon after, a family home was built across the road. When the factory fell on hard times in the 1940s, someone bought the Inn and moved it north 5 miles and converted it to a cottage on Lake DuBay. Our family bought the cheesemaker's house in 1979. Soon after, I found the remnants of a brick foundation where the Inn sat across the road. The old brick factory still stands, but has lost the test of time and is now crumbling. Today, when flies and birds fly by, they carry the echoes of farmers, passerby's and children - gleefully munching, chugging and licking.

August 26

Cool weather and low humidity beckoned us to the kennel deck yesterday where we greeted the coming of fall, while enjoying one of the fleeting days of summer passing by. It was 48 degrees this morning. We heard the grandkids playing in the woods across the road, smelled an afternoon campfire as their parents grilled hamburgers and brats. And at dusk, we watched a woodcock flying low along the edge of the field. Life is good!

MUSIC TO MY EARS

A pair of geese fly by honking,
Bobwhites whistling from the prairie grass,
Nesting cranes trumpeting in the marsh,
A woodcock sky dancing by the hedgerow,
Male cardinals whistling from treetop high,
Robins caroling on the kennel lawn,
Pileated woodpeckers rattling deep in the woods,
White-throated sparrows thrilled whistles.
A late summer symphony nearly everyday,
and music to my ears.

September 1

Opening day. In my world, it's the Glorious First of September. Across the Atlantic Ocean, in Great Britain and Northern Ireland, the start of shooting season for their famous red grouse is celebrated as the Glorious Twelfth. The twelfth day of August is celebrated by legislation in England and Wales. No legislative act here in our state for September 1st. Our Glorious First is celebrated by those of us that have waited patiently for our favorite time of the year. And I declare it a holiday in my world view.

September 4

It's that time of the year. Late summer, early fall family trips means a full house at our boarding kennel. Keeps me close to home, but allows for some quality time hunting over decoys for geese and doves on our fields out back. Local birds are far and few between, but enough to keep things interesting. Nighthawks sweep by late in the afternoon on their annual journey south.

September 7

A drive-about hunt at nearby Mead and Paul Carson wildlife areas fed food for the soul, but nothing for the game bag. Saw plenty of both doves and geese, but none while actually hunting. Scouting for new areas to hunt once the rest of the seasons, like grouse, pheasant and woodcock open in a few weeks is also a wonderful pastime.

September 14

Mid-month hunting near our place along the creek has taken on a new meaning as I enter a new phase in the evolution of a hunter. Those in the know have dissected the different phases of a hunter's life. New and young participants are driven by bag limits. Mid-life hunters savor the guns, dogs and equipment they can afford and need to satisfy their urge to spend time in the woods and marshes. Towards the end of their hunting life cycle, it's time to smell the roses, scratch their dog on the head and sit in the blind with a gun across their lap. My life as a hunter has taken on that phase. Waiting for geese, doves and deer on our back 40 stirs my senses these days like hunting in the Dakotas and Canada did back years ago.

September 22

The leaves of autumn are turning shades of red, yellow and orange. Frost has transformed ground vegetation into fuel for soil. Woodcock and wood ducks are stirring for fall migration. October is knocking at the door.

"October is a month made for Wisconsin bird hunters. It's a scene filled with golden popple stands, walking ankle deep in leaves on the forest floor and watching grouse thundering out of red dogwood patches. Add a hunting dog, a golden brown cattail marsh and a cornfield, and watch an upland hunter's pulse quicken. Give me October twelve months of the year and I'll know what heaven's all about."
~Ken M.Blomberg, Badger Sportsman, 1992. Passages - The Greatest Quotations From Sporting Literature - Sporting Classics.

October 4

A trip to Maine this week into next. On an airplane for the first time in a long time. Instead of five days or more on the road coming and going, we chose to fly and cut the travel time down to two days. That allowed for more time spent in Maine with No. 1 son Erik, his wife Sabrina and grandson No. 2.

October 5

Years ago, when working for a living, I met Wisconsin State Senator Neal Kedzie at an affair in Madison where he was keynote speaker at a water resource conference. We chatted over a cup of coffee during a break and to our amazements, we discovered the house my family lives in along the creek was built by his grandfather in the 1920s. That, and the cheese factory across the street from our house. He followed up by visiting one summer day last year to take pictures and reminisce about his childhood memories of days spent visiting his grandparents living here on Mayflower Road.

October 6

Today, I received the following story entitled, A Short History of Mayflower Cheese Factory, est. 1922 by Neal Kedzie, Middleton, WI

"My Grandfather (my dad's dad) was Stanislaw "Stanley" Kadzielawski (1888-1953). He was born in Poland to a farming family. Due to the family facing financial hardship, he left home at the age of 16 to seek his fame and fortune and signed up as a crewman on a merchant ship in hope of reaching America. He eventually landed in Chicago in 1905. In pursuit of the American dream, he learned various trades over the years while seeking his niche, including; a butcher, cabinet maker and tailor. His future wife, Anna (Horowicz) was also born in Poland (1889-1974) and immigrated to Chicago in 1905, where she had relatives living. The couple met and later married in Chicago in 1917.

"Sometime around 1920-21, Stanley invested in a potato warehouse operation somewhere in the Central Sands Region of Wisconsin. Word later got back to him,after the potato harvest, that the warehouse burned down and the entire crop was destroyed. He decided to drive his Model T Ford to Central Wisconsin to see the damage for himself. As it turned out, the warehouse had burned but there was no sign of any potatoes ever having been stored there. Stanley lost his entire investment to a scam. Stanley was drawn to the terrain of Central Wisconsin, since it reminded him of his homeland. Being an entrepreneur, he decided to turn a negative experience into a positive. He had heard that the region had a growing cheese industry that was sourced from numerous local dairy herds, so he decided to make another career change – cheesemaker.

"He searched for land to purchase around Stevens Point where he could build a cheese factory as well as a house for his soon-to-be growing family. He settled on the Town of Eau Pleine. After the cheese factory was built, Stanley decided to name it the Mayflower Cheese Factory, after the numerous May flower plants that bloomed each spring in the nearby woods and for the Mayflower ship that brought the first immigrants to America, since he too was an immigrant. He hired a master cheesemaker to teach him the art of cheesemaking. Their primary cheeses were Colby and cheddar. The factory and house had no electricity until after WWII and ran on a wood-fired boiler and utilized kerosene lamps. Every year my grandfather would purchase part of a wood lot and have the local saw mill rip the logs for future fuel to be used to feed the boiler. Block ice was cut from the nearby Wisconsin River each winter for refrigeration and delivered by horse drawn sleds. Cheesemaking was a family affair, with my grandmother, and later the children, all pitching in.

"My grandparents had four children. Lillian (b.1981) was the oldest and was the first to attend college at Stevens Point. After college she taught at the one-room local schoolhouse. Julia (b.1921) went on to serve as Postmistress for Junction City. Alex (b.1925), my father, served as a milk hauler and picked up milk cans from the local dairy farmers. He went off to fight in WWII, graduated from Marquette University on the G.I. Bill, and had a career in business in the Milwaukee area. Henry "Hank" (b.1928) was the baby who stayed home to keep the cheese factory running with his father during and after the war.

"Following my grandfather's death, Henry moved to Junction City with my grandmother and cared for her for the rest of her life. He never married. He was a volunteer firefighter for 35 years, very active in the JC Lions Club and worked at the Wisconsin Rapids paper mill until his retirement. The Mayflower Cheese Factory was sold by my grandfather around 1950 because of his declining health due to heart disease. He was so disappointed in the way that the new party was running the operation that he bought it back. After Stanley passed away, my uncle Hank eventually sold the cheese factory for the final time in the middle 1950's. It ceased operation as a cheese factory and was used for various purposes, including a bleach manufacturing business and later for storage."

October 22

Two small flocks of Canada geese flew over my field decoys while I fed dogs and cleaned kennels around 9 am. I better get done with chores and get down to my blind post haste!

October 23

Sitting for geese and doves in the pines at the end of the

114

prairie field. Unseasonably warm south westerly winds. 9:05 am - high incoming dove overhead. Missed. 9:10 am - immature bald Eagle flew over my backside and south towards golden pond. Constant chatter of flocks of blackbirds going nowhere fast. Seems to be satisfied sharing time between the neighbor's cornfield and Vera's Pond's cattails. Eating, drinking and preparing for their migration south. 9:57 am - turned a flock of geese east flying south towards my decoys. About30 in number, several cupped their wings but swung southeast over the creek and out of range. Good thing my blood pressure medication is working fine! 10:17 am - several more flocks of geese flew overhead. 2 shots. Either they were just out of reach, or my lead was off. My guess is the latter.

CLOSE YOUR EYES

*Close your eyes and
think.
From the front lobe of
your brain, pull it out.
Fond memories lost
to time, but fresh if
brought out of storage.
Close your eyes and
think hard.*

*Of the time I bought
my first bird dog puppy
near Shawano.
The first grouse camp fire
I shared with friends
up north.*

Fathers Day weekend
gatherings at the kennel
with family and friends.
Bringing my first cocker
Buster home from Hilbert.

November 21

Of all the birds that frequent our feeders, it's the Black-capped Chickadees that steal the show for me. Collectively, the colorful portrait outside our kitchen window includes more dramatic red male cardinals, rowdy blue jays and black, white and sometimes red woodpeckers. But hands down, my favorite bird is the Chickadee – a feathered friend that years ago led me to two most interesting fellows.

Bold by nature, these small, energetic birds are about 5 inches long, black capped, black bibbed and sport a pair of white cheeks. For those with time and patience, they can be persuaded to take a sunflower seed from an extended hand. It was that trait that led me to appreciate fellow number one - the grandfather of a college buddy that lived up north in the woods near Monico.

"Grandpa" had a flock of tame Chickadees working his living room window feeder and he was proud to show them off. He spoke of them with delight, as he did the flying squirrels that visited each evening - the spotlight we bought had brought them closer to his world. During the day, with nothing but time on his hands, he had patiently conditioned his birds to feed from hand. The secret to his success involved cracking the sunflower shells and exposing the edible kernel. He insisted, "Take a handful and try for yourself."

To experience a living creature weighing 1/3 of an ounce balanced weightlessly on your hand, is to appreciate the saying, "lighter than air". The birds that dared to eat from my hand that day did so with gusto, as the prediction for cold temperatures were in the forecast. When temperatures drop to zero degrees Fahrenheit the Chickadee must consume up to 60% of its body weight in food. For a person weighing 200 pounds, that would translate into nearly 120 pounds of groceries!

Away from the bird feeders and deep in the woods, a Chickadee's diet consists of insects, insect eggs, spiders, spider eggs, berries and small seeds from pine cones. During the cold months of winter, they locate hidden food they've stored under the bark and cracks of trees and branches deep in the woods. That's where I met fellow number two – the late, great ornithologist, Don "Fuzz" Follen of Arpin.

Back in the early 1980's, Don literally took me by the hand and led me deeper into the wonderful world of birds and bird banding. I followed him across flowages to band osprey, up trees to band several species of owls and even across the state to find the elusive Great Gray Owl. Don taught me to question the unknown and his home in the swamp was a perfect setting for exploring nature's mysteries. From his window he pondered one day after watching a steady flow of Chickadees coming to his feeders. Finally, he remarked, "There's no way the same birds are eating all the sunflower seeds we put out."

So he started an aggressive banding program that would count and mark the birds, one at a time. He gave up after tagging well over a hundred birds, noting that they must come and go from long distances to his feeding station. They didn't all belong to his backyard flock. As it turned out, Don had experienced a major fall chickadee flight – a minor invasion which established the winter territories of the birds near his home on the edge of a rather large swamp.

Our feeders along the creek aren't an attraction for a flight of these tiny bundles of energy, but we get our share. Time and patience aren't in the cards these days, but some day, not too far around the corner, I plan on cracking some seeds and handing out a few kernels to the willing. And all I'll ask in return is a few cheerful "chick-a-dee-dees".

November 30

Another deer hunting season has come and gone here along the creek. The Zandi boys, father Craig and son Josh and my great grandnephew Quinn were here once again. For more than forty years, my sons and close friends have shared this magical week at the end of November. I have lost count of the number of deer we have harvested over the years. But the memories remain stored in my mind forever.

December 9

One of our trail cameras ran low on batteries, so I took the big John Deere tractor to Golden Pond to reactivate it. That was at 2:39 pm. At 2:43 pm, 4 minutes after I left, a small buck appeared and triggered the camera. That said, and the five does and fawns that stood their ground as I passed by, told me how tolerant deer are of humans sitting on motorized vehicles.

DEAD TREES AND BRUSH PILES

Dead trees in our backyard are very much alive.
Alive with resident birds making a living harvesting
dormant insects lodged under peeling rotten bark.
Woodpeckers, nuthatches, chickadees and bluejays
visit often, poking and prodding every last morsel
this avian smorgasbord has to offer hungry creatures.

Our rural estate is no Better Home and Garden candidate.
Unless they expand contest guidelines to include dead, dying
and crumbling vegetation. Brown grass and tangled copses
in all directions lend themselves to an unkept landscape.
It matters not to the birds and creatures that call it home.
Home is where thirst, hunger and the need to rest leads them.

So backyard dead trees and that which litter our back 40 are crucial
for the survival of living things that truly own the land we live on.
As we speak, a small herd of deer feed on their winter diet of
woody vegetation - preferring the treetops of last winter's clearcut.
A trio of Pileated woodpeckers carve away at dead standing timber
and rabbits living in brush piles provide supper for resident foxes.

Our dead trees and brush piles are indeed alive.

Several trips to town these days to be entertained by our grandchildren at their school winter concerts and plays. Last night's pre-kindergarten show with grandson Rykar, who just turned 4, was outstanding. Onstage with his classmates in a packed auditorium at the Catholic high school was quite impressive, as were performances from his older sister and brother. Talent here runs deep.

CAN YOU?

Can you smell the landscape?
Prairies smell different
than piney woods,
which smell different
than aspen woods or
oak covered ridge-lines,
or alder bottoms,
or October cornfields.

Can you feel Nature's wet,
dew drenched grasses on the trail,
frost covered woodland ferns,
thorny briars on a thicket edge,
bitter northwest winds and frozen
water crystals on your cheeks?

Can you hear seasonal sounds
of fall migrant birds,

approaching winter snowstorms,
spring mating melodies,
and late summer thunderstorms?.

Can you see
the forest for the trees,
cotton ball clouds against blue skies,
newborn creatures of the year,
insects on the pond's surface
being swallowed by hungry fish
and tadpoles sprouting legs?

Can you taste
flavors of the seasons,
like fresh wild spring asparagus,
summer sweet corn on the cob,
autumn's pumpkin and squash
and a mouthful of fresh snow?

If you can,
then you understand.

December 19

Willie Nelson just celebrated his 90th birthday. I had the great pleasure of meeting him years ago on a small commercial airplane ride from Chicago into central Wisconsin. After giving me his autograph, he asked me to walk with him from the plane through the airport to a van waiting to transport him to the Marathon County fairgrounds where he was performing that evening. Can you imagine the number of words he has blended with songs over the years? Beyond belief, I am sure. Words put to print or paired with music, are gifts artists like Nelson share with us all. I heard one of his sons perform and sing with him recently. If you close your eyes, it's hard to tell the difference between the two. Johnny Cash's grandson also performs these days and echoes his grandfather's voice. Their gifts live on.

December 21

Two semi loads of pulp passed by the house this morning. Red pine in 8-foot lengths, small and less than 8 inches in diameter. Destined for a nearby paper mill. No doubt cut from the 1500 acres of paper mill land along River Road north of our place. If they don't replant the harvested spot with more pine, it'll revert to aspen, oak and locust. Ruffed grouse, woodcock, deer and other young forest wildlife hope for the latter.

December 24

Awaiting a white Christmas. With unseasonably warm temperatures for the foreseeable future it's highly unlikely.

December 29

Death came to our township this week. A neighbor's 3-year old grandchild died in a tragic farming accident. A young woman was killed in a head-on collision on nearby Highway 10. And a township employee lost his life during a stump removal operation.

December 30

A neighborhood raven flew over our house this morning. I heard him long before he came into view. His raucous call contained strange gurgling sounds I'd never heard before. How many vocalizations (words) do ravens have in their vocabulary?

The goose season officially closed today south of Highway 10. North of that line it ended last month on the 16th. An occasional flock or two still flies by these days, but until spring arrives, their honks will soon cease. When winter turns to spring their music will return to our stretch of the Wisconsin River Valley.

WONDER WHY?

I saw a bald eagle flying over the clinic
in town yesterday.
Then I saw my doctor fly over my chart at the clinic.
The eagle simply glided past on a northwest wind looking for food,
My doctor stopped when looking at my cholesterol levels.
Why was the eagle heading north?
Why did my cholesterol levels head north?
The eagle was hungry.
I, in turn, inadvertently forgot my daily pills for a spell.
The eagle hadn't eaten for days.
Off to the drug store for this patient today.
I'll bet the eagle's blood work is just fine.

A flock of turkeys passed over the gravel road where the creek crosses at the end of our back 40. It's been a fairly easy winter so far and based on the neighborhood turkey numbers, things look promising for area wildlife. But there's plenty of winter days left until spring.

January 5

Leopold described ecology in terms of animal economics. He dissected a creature's home range by season, by food and cover and defense from predators. A rabbit flushed by his dog Gus during the winter showed Leopold the path of that rabbit's estate. "A beeline for a woodpile a quarter-mile distant" showed the rabbit's home range was at the very least that far in extent. He also observed chickadees, deer, and grouse in his Sand County Almanac essay Home Range.

"One cannot know intimately all the ways and movements of a river without growing to love it."
~Roderick Haig-Brown

January 11

Leopold's Sand County Almanac essay January Thaw described nights of thaw. Midwinter warming that awakens hibernating creatures in the woods and grasslands. Skunks wake and wander across-country, meadow mice abroad in daylight and in turn, hawks searching for the now vulnerable rodents. That was in the 1940s. I wonder what he'd say about the winter of 2023-24? Warmer than ever. The warmest December in history. It wasn't until mid-January that fishermen dared to drill into the ice. Measurable snow finally arrived two nights ago and last night. Used our snowblower for the first time this winter.

Watched the grandkids ice skating in town this afternoon at the city's indoor rink. Young Ryker asked if we could snow skate when we got home - now that we have snow on the ground. "Snow skate?" I asked. "Yes Papa," he replied. "Nina has snow skates in the garden shed." "Oh, do you mean snowshoes?" "Yep Papa, snow skates."

When it's minus one degree outside, soft boiled eggs are good comfort food. That, and a couple of donut holes and some cottage cheese with chives to start the day. The boss did morning kennel chores this morning while the grandkids watched cartoons near the warm pellet stove. I did kennel chores last evening and spared the kids the task due to colder than normal temperatures.

WINTER ARRIVED JUST LIKE THAT

Ten below and I feel like waiting.
Waiting for winds to shift from north to south.
From clockwise to counterclockwise.
From wind chill danger,
To gentle warming trends.

Snow and ice now cover our neck of the world.
Turning the landscape winter white.
Making our backyard birds busier than normal.
Feeding non-stop on store bought seeds and suet.
Causing the back 40 deer herd to browse woody vegetation.

Friends Jimmy and Dan measure their favorite lakes not by number of fish,
but by inches of ice produced each night by below zero temperatures.
"I got on ice today," said Dan last week. " 5 inches on Prairie Lake.
Just a small perch so far.
The rest of the lakes are open, you could use your boat. "
This week's attic blast will change that in a heartbeat.

And so it goes. Winter arrived just like that. Now we wait.
Wait for winds to shift from north to south.
From clockwise to counterclockwise.
From wind chill danger to gentle warming trends.
Then watch for signs of spring.

Greeted with a rejection email this morning from an Ohio publisher of my fourth book, Country Journal and Old Man's Musings. Looking around for other potential publishers as my Wisconsin based one is currently reorganizing and not accepting new manuscripts.

Oh well, Shannon, the publisher of two of my first three books replied to another email I sent yesterday. Gave me the go ahead despite her publishing company's recent pause in accepting submissions. "Yes, I would love to review your manuscript. You have secret VIP access to our submissions when they are closed. Just email it to me!". I guess it's not always what you know, but who you know.

GETTING OLDER

By the second,
60 clicks and we're another minute older.
By the minute,
Again, 60 clicks and another hour has past.
By the hour,
24 clicks and a day goes by.
355 more, and a new year is on our doorstep.
10 years and another decade passes us by.
Life only allows for 8, or if we're lucky, 10 decades at the most.
So… count your seconds as blessings.

January 23

No. 2 grandson, Carson celebrated his seventh birthday today. He lives with his folks in the great state of Maine. Near Old Towne, where the famous canoes are made. Mountains in the northwest and an ocean on the east coast. Home of moose, deer and grouse and creatures like sea lions, whales, lobsters, clams and puffins. Ponds (they don't use the term lakes) and rivers galore, where he and his father fish throughout the year. I must dust off my fishing gear this year, I dare say that young boy catches more than his dear old Papa these days.

January 24

Speaking of grandchildren, No. 1 and only granddaughter is now playing basketball. She's in 5th grade and has taken to this sport after a successful season of volleyball. Grandmother and I enjoy attending the games and cheering them on. At this stage, it is more of a learning experience, and while the score is kept, it's not stressed. Everyone wins as they gain beginner's experience. The looks on the faces of parents and grandparents on the sidelines is priceless.

January 29

Good news Monday! From my Wisconsin publisher. "Hello Ken, Our team reviewed your manuscript. It is so well written as always! I have attached their feedback form, and they suggested we offer you a contract for publication." Country Journal and Old Man Musings will go to print this year.

January 30

When we're closer to the end than the beginning we often think of loved ones from the past. Parents, siblings, in-laws, aunts, uncles and grandparents. Genealogy becomes an endearing pastime. The history of family and insights into their character fill in the gaps, allowing us to know what makes us tick.

"Death steals everything except our stories."
~Jim Harrison, In Search of Small Gods

WHEN I PASS

When you lay me to rest,
leave on my vest,
boots on my feet,
and some change in my pockets.

If you choose cremation, that's alright.
The garb and coin will follow my
spirit into the Beyond.
If not, bury me deep.

Below the frost line.
You know I don't like the cold,
that chill on my bones from head to toes.
Perhaps warmth from cremation is a better choice.

Into the Beyond I will go,
where my father, grandfathers
and kin wait by the edge of the
Great Forest alongside my pack of dogs.

Together we will rejoice.
Walking hand in hand, following
our trusted canine companions
through forever golden uplands.

Ella Wilcox told grandfather Ivan over his grave,
"Death is but a crossing, a little strip of sea,
to find one's loved ones waiting on the shore.
More beautiful, more precious than before.

The Beyond; home of those of whom I am so fond."

February 1

Sap in maple trees is running! In fact, before the end of January this year, area maple syrup producers began tapping their trees, as unseasonably warm days and frosty nights fooled sap into flowing more than a month early. Ice fishing tournaments are being canceled and sturgeon spearing seasons are now in jeopardy. Everything is lopsided this season. Last week bucks on our back 40 were still in rut, chasing does. Ice is going out on the lakes and they're catching walleyes on open water on the River. A reliable source and his pointing dog told us a woodcock is back on the Mead - while surprising, not totally out of the question. And if we get smacked with snow later this month, we know woodcock can and will reverse migrate south. With a good tailwind, here today, mid-Illinois tomorrow!

February 2

Groundhogs in Pennsylvania and Wisconsin both failed to see their shadows this morning. So as the saying goes, an early spring is at hand. Yep, it seems to be here already!

"All art is but an imitation of nature."
~Lucius Seneca

February 5

A stretch of fifty-degree weather greets us this week. Neighbors on Dam Road saw a nightcrawler and frog on the blacktop past their home. A robin was spotted near our Rhinelander friend's home late last week. I thought I heard one in the woods behind the kennels yesterday, but could not verify that fact. However, there's no doubt in my mind that a male cardinal belted out his spring love song near our house today.

February 7

This winter will go down in history as record-breaking. Record warm days. Record low snow falls. And so on. Lakes froze over, only to reopen in January. It's the second week of February and fields across the state are bare. This coming spring may harbor dry ground cover and severe fire danger. The Wisconsin River passing through our neighborhood is open wide, bank to bank. Trucks pulling trailered boats head to Dam Road to cash in on an early walleye run. I must drive along River Road today, just to see it for myself once more.

February 8

Thirty-five wild turkeys strolled by the clearcut trail camera early this morning. While lingering long enough for a multitude of pictures, they gathered their share of abundant acorns, now easily plucked off the snow free forest floor. Our back 40 wildlife residents are doing famously during this gentle winter.

February 9

These things I ponder while waiting for spring to arrive. Temperatures have risen prematurely. Will May flowers bloom in April? Will yellow marsh-marigold sprout on schedule along the creek bottom this year? How about the early migrant birds? Who will show up first above our prairie-grass field? And bluebirds. Will we see more than one pair this year? A few more nesting boxes are in order.

February 10

Two large bucks followed three does past the Golden Pond trail cam last night. Still sporting full racks of antlers, they spared for five minutes over the affections of the nearby ladies. Tonight, the larger of the two bucks returned, as did the female deer, tell-ing me the big guy won the battle. Looking for shed antlers on our property with the grandkids this spring should be rewarding.

February 12

I look out my kennel office window over the prairie grass field, still standing strong during the last month of winter. There is no sign of snow on the landscape, which explains the fall-like look to this picture. Our Back 40 deer herd emerge from the woods each evening, graze in the food plot, cross the hedgerow and make their way across the gravel road to spend the night on the neighbor's 80 acres of harvested soybean and corn fields. Oh, what an easy time our resident wildlife have had this time around the sun.

"The season's first bluebird chortled and sang along the brook this afternoon. How welcome were his notes in the thawing landscape! All around were the voices of winter - crow caws, junco and sparrow song, the challenge of a pileated woodpecker, jay scolding, the cries of woodpeckers and the 'phe-be-be' of chickadees - only the bluebird announced the vernal season."
~August Derleth - Countryman's Journal

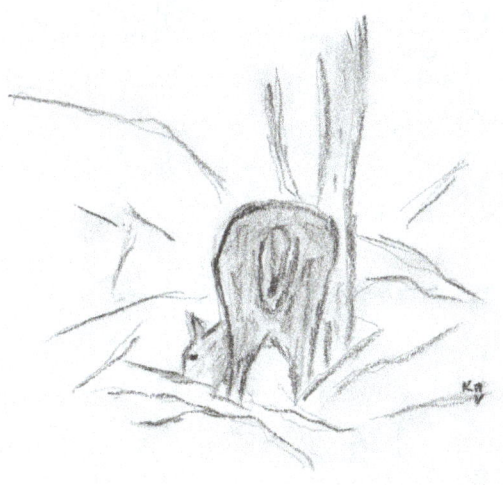

SPRING RETURNS

I took to the river for a while today, to look for spring who had left us a day or three ago, to places Mother Nature only knows.

There she was, spring, hidden in the sparkling ripples, peeking down at me through scattered clouds, riding on a gentle southeasterly breeze, and teasing me into thinking she was truly on her way back home.

Piles of snow from the township plow lay along River Road and lead me back to our gravel driveway. March mud clings to my boots, the dog's paws and the boss's brand new SUV. The boots and dogs remain at the kennel, while I take a stand on the kennel deck.

From my perch I patiently wait for early spring migrants to come out of hiding. The pair of cranes trumpet from the neighbor's picked cornfield. Robins dash across the lawn looking for worms along edges of puddles. Blackbirds chatter from the cattail choked ponds, while passing gulls cry for their mates on the way to DuBay.

www.ingramcontent.com/pod-product-compliance
Lightning Source LLC
Chambersburg PA
CBHW060331260626
47160CB00007B/2772